# DAIRY-FREE COOKBOOK FOR KIDS

# DAIRY-FREE
## COOKBOOK *for kids*
### 100 RECIPES FOR BUSY FAMILIES

**DANIELLE FAHRENKRUG**

PHOTOGRAPHY BY MARIJA VIDAL

ROCKRIDGE
PRESS

Interior and Cover Designer: Elizabeth Zuhl
Art Producer: Janice Ackerman
Production Editor: Andrew Yackira
Photography: © 2020 Marija Vidal. Food styling by Victoria Woollard.

ISBN: Print 978-1-64611-622-5 | eBook 978-1-64611-623-2
R0

This book is dedicated to my children, Chase and Curren.

You are my biggest accomplishment in life and I love you.

May you continue to thrive and grow into incredibly

wonderful, talented, and smart humans.

Thank you for your help in choosing favorite recipes

and taste testing them for this cookbook for all to enjoy.

# contents

# introduction

Life with children is wonderful, even if it is busy and, at times, a bit topsy-turvy. If you have a child with a dairy intolerance, the happy chaos of family life can be punctuated by worry and frustration about how to feed them. After all, kids can be notoriously picky eaters and having to remove dairy from the equation can make mealtimes feel overwhelming. This feeling may be the reason you've turned to this book. If so, you've come to the right place! As a mother of a child with dairy intolerance, I have been where you are now, and I'm here to help.

When we started a family, our days of leisure and little responsibility ended and a whole new life of hustle, joy, purpose, and love blossomed. In the first moment I held my firstborn, I remember looking in his eyes and promising to do whatever it took to protect him and give him the opportunities he needed to thrive. I could not believe how much love poured over me that day.

Fast-forward five years to a trip to a doughnut shop where my son was drinking dairy milk. Shortly afterward, he was throwing up. The same thing had happened when he ate bread with cream cheese. If that was not frightening enough, there were additional symptoms that came with eating dairy: He would lash out in tantrums with uncharacteristic anger. I was in tears trying to find ways to help him.

I hear similar stories all the time: Parents in a constant state of worry, trying to figure out what is causing their children to have migraines, frequent stomachaches, lack of focus, and fits of anger. Oftentimes, the cause is a food allergy or intolerance, one of the most common of which is dairy intolerance.

When we started to make sense of my son's symptoms, we already ate mostly dairy free and gluten free. I began to notice a definite pattern when I added dairy to his diet. We then started eliminating dairy and gluten completely, which helped ease my son's irrational behaviors, and he stopped getting sick.

Adapting to new ways of looking at and enjoying food are the first steps to a happy dairy-free lifestyle. Eliminating milk products from your diet can be challenging in the beginning, but with some helpful kid-friendly recipes and a little time, I promise, it gets easier. Taste buds start to change and these easy dairy-free recipes will become a part of a lifestyle.

As my pastor put it, "Life is a little salty and a little sweet—like a maple-glazed bacon doughnut," and as with everything sweet, the salty makes the sweet moments even sweeter. For me, the "saltiness" of my kids' food sensitivities put me on a "sweet" journey to develop delicious healthy recipes that ensure kids don't feel like they are missing out. Then, I started blogging to share these recipes with others who were going through the same thing. I am so happy that, through the years, my recipes have helped thousands of parents create meals that bring nutrition and smiles to all ages! You can visit my blog at *DelightfulMomFood.com*.

I have specially created 100 dairy-free recipes for this book that are not only kid friendly but also family friendly, because no one wants to cook more than one meal at mealtime. I have included some family favorites, such as macaroni and cheese and taquitos (no animal cheese required!). To make your dairy-free journey easier, many recipes can be completed in under 1 hour, and some can even be made in advance for wholesome and energizing treats on the go. The recipes don't require an extensive list of ingredients—everything in this book is affordable and simple, as life should be. There is even a primer on dairy-free living that details ingredients used throughout this book.

The possibilities are endless with dairy-free cooking the whole family can enjoy. Thank you for letting me join you on your journey toward becoming a happy, healthy, dairy-free family.

**TURKEY TACO BOWLS WITH FRESH GUACAMOLE, PAGE 118**

*chapter one*

# THE DAIRY-FREE FAMILY

Eating dairy free as a family can be easy and delicious, but it does require a little learning curve in the beginning. I am here to help you learn. In this chapter, I cover the basics of dairy; the difference between dairy intolerance and milk allergies; and how to identify sneaky milk products on food labels. With a little knowledge and some adjustments, your family will be on the road to a happy, healthy, dairy-free lifestyle in no time.

# WHAT IS DAIRY-FREE?

When beginning your journey to select, cook, and eat dairy-free foods, you need to know which foods and food products contain dairy and which are dairy free. Traditional dairy products, including butter, cheese, ice cream, milk, and yogurt, contain the milk proteins and milk sugar (lactose) that cause dairy allergies and intolerances. But where else could milk products be lurking?

You may be surprised to learn that dairy is found in a vast array of food products. It can be found in cereal bars, chocolate chips, granola bars, sauces, salad dressings, and even gluten-free flour mixes. Milk protein is also present in anything made with casein, caseinates, and whey, and lactose is used to make baked goods moist and soft.

To make things more confusing, the prevalence of dairy means its language can infiltrate the names of food products that do not contain dairy, such as shea butter, cocoa butter, and coconut butter as well as cream of tartar. And what about eggs, which are often lumped together with milk products in the dairy case? Are food items with eggs, such as marshmallows, mayonnaise, and fresh pasta, off the menu?

The good news is, many items use the terminology of dairy products to convey common characteristics, such as the spreadability of butter, though they are, in fact, safe for people who exclude dairy from their diet. And, if you picture eggs as dairy, you are not alone. But eggs do not contain milk proteins or lactose, so they are not true dairy products. Therefore, eggs are allowed within this diet, provided your child does not have an egg allergy.

Although at first eliminating dairy may seem challenging, knowing which foods are dairy free—and having plenty of alternatives for those that aren't—makes coping with your child's dairy allergy or intolerance much easier.

# DAIRY-FREE FOR BETTER HEALTH

Understanding the differences between having lactose intolerance and a milk allergy is the first step in taking charge of your new dairy-free life. Although genetics play a big part in our lives, they do not determine our destiny. A dairy-free diet has many health benefits and relieves many unnecessary discomforts.

## Lactose Intolerance

Lactose is a naturally occurring sugar found in milk and milk products. It makes up from 2 percent to 8 percent of milk and provides a mildly sweet taste.

According to the National Dairy Council, the inability to break down lactose, due to a deficiency or lack of the enzyme lactase, is known as lactose intolerance. Symptoms of lactose intolerance, such as an upset stomach, abdominal pain, bloating, congestion, diarrhea, and agitation (specifically in children), occur after eating or drinking dairy. A lactose intolerance is not the same as a milk allergy, because *it does not involve the immune system*.

Consult a doctor if you think your child may be lactose intolerant. Your doctor may recommend removing dairy from a child's diet to see if symptoms disappear. The doctor may follow removing dairy with a hydrogen breath test or blood test to test sugar, which would confirm a diagnosis. Treatment options include enzyme supplementation, eating lactose-free foods, or eliminating dairy altogether. The best course of action for your family will depend on your child's individual symptoms. Luckily, there is a variety of lactose-free foods available and the recipes in this book offer lots of options that will make your child happier and more comfortable!

## Milk Allergy

A *milk allergy* is an *immune system* reaction to milk protein, which can be life threatening. It differs from lactose intolerance, which is when the body can't digest the milk sugar found in milk products. Symptoms of a milk allergy may include vomiting, hives, difficulty breathing, and even anaphylaxis, which requires immediate medical attention.

If you suspect that your child has a milk allergy, consult a doctor. Your doctor or allergist may conduct a skin-prick test, a blood test, or an oral challenge test (this should be done only under medical supervision). Treatment will include the elimination of dairy foods, which requires reading labels on all foods closely. If your child's symptoms are severe, your doctor will likely also prescribe an epinephrine auto-injector to use in case of emergencies.

If a child has a cow's-milk allergy, they should avoid all milk products, including foods labeled lactose free, as well as other animal milks, such as goat's and sheep's milk. Any food product that lists casein, galactose, ghee, or whey on its label contains milk and should be avoided.

## Plant-Based Diet

A diet rich in plants is the answer to enjoying "dairy" again. In this book you will find satisfying versions of homemade plant-based milks (see chapter 2), Queso Dipping Cheese (page 170), and Homemade Shredding Cheese (page 174) made of plant-based oils and nuts instead of milk proteins. Use these vegan milks and cheeses in creamy pasta dishes, grilled cheese sandwiches, and quesadillas, or to top salads. Nutrients lost when avoiding milk are calcium, phosphorus, protein, riboflavin, and vitamin D, which can all be obtained through other sources. Some of those sources include fortified drinks and cereals, leafy greens, legumes, tofu, and whole grains, all of which play a role in fueling the body and provide lasting energy.

# BIG 8 FOOD ALLERGIES

Did you know that 90 percent of food allergies in the United States are caused by eight major allergenic foods referred to as the Big 8? These foods include the following:

| MILK | EGGS | FISH | SHELLFISH |
| TREE NUTS | PEANUTS | WHEAT | SOY |

The American Academy of Allergy, Asthma, and Immunology notes that 6 percent to 8 percent of children have food allergies and, of those, about 30 percent have multiple food allergies. According to the Food Allergy Research and Resource Program (FARRP) at the University of Nebraska, allergies that are relatively common in infancy and childhood include allergies to eggs, milk, soybeans, and wheat. Milk allergies are the most common among those, occurring in 2 percent to 6 percent of young children.

Each recipe in this book has labels that let you know at a glance if it is safe for people with other Big 8 food allergies, and those that are completely Big 8 allergen free are labeled "Allergen-Free."

# READING FOOD LABELS

One of the most important things you can do if your child has dairy intolerance or a milk allergy is read food labels. Even if you believe the product you're buying does not have milk in it, the safest practice is still to check the label.

The US Food and Drug Administration requires all food labels on products that contain any milk or milk proteins to notify the consumer somewhere on the packaging that it does contain "milk." Some labels may also say "made in a facility that processes milk," which means that cross-contamination may have occurred in a facility or on equipment shared with products that include dairy.

Milk can be found in surprising things such as natural flavoring, caramel flavoring, high-protein flour, lactic acid (usually not a problem), and lactic acid starter culture. Look out for these sneaky alternate terms.

Even if the packaging makes claims that look appealing, you should still read the ingredient label carefully. One of our favorite cheese alternatives is one from Trader Joe's made of almonds and it comes shredded. In small print at the top of the packaging, it says "99 percent lactose free." The ingredient label lists milk powder. For some, this small amount of milk product will not harm them, but for someone with a high intolerance or allergy, even 1 percent can cause havoc.

Ultimately, let the ingredients, not the marketing, speak for the product. The best way to triumph over confusing packaged goods is to educate yourself. To learn more about food labels, check out the resources section at the end of this book.

## Dairy-Free versus Nondairy

As you read labels, it's important to have some background on the terms *dairy free* and *nondairy,* which are often used on food packaging. According to FARRP, the word *dairy free* does not have a regulatory definition. Therefore, companies may use the term in different ways. For example, they may use the label to indicate the absence of certain types of milk products, but still make the item with milk derivatives. *Nondairy* does have a regulatory definition; however, the definition allows caseins to be used in the making of the product. Some "nondairy" products that may contain casein include rice cheese and soy cheese. So, once again, the best way to ensure that the product you're buying is without dairy of any kind is to read the ingredient label.

To eliminate your worry about whether a food does or does not have dairy, I provide six homemade plant-based milk recipes in chapter 2 that are 100 percent free of artificial ingredients and dairy. Also, for the recipes in this book, I use the term "dairy free" to indicate that an ingredient should have no milk, milk proteins, or milk derivatives on the ingredient label.

## Words to Watch For

**CASEIN:** Casein is used as a major component of cheese and as a food additive, and the most common way it is listed on food labels is *sodium caseinate*.

**LACTOSE:** Lactose is found is traditional dairy foods, such as butter, cheese, cream, ice cream, milk, and yogurt, but it also pops up in seemingly random processed foods, such as baked goods, candy, cookies, crackers, deli meats, drink mixes, margarine, salad dressings, sauces, and soups.

**WHEY:** Dried whey is found in protein bars and energy drinks and the liquid form is in cheese and yogurt.

### Other Ingredients that Could Spell Trouble

- Caramel flavoring
- Custard
- Flavoring
- Galactose
- High-protein flour
- Natural flavoring
- Nisin preparation
- Nougat
- Protein hydrolysate
- Pudding
- Quark
- Recaldent
- Rennet
- Simplesse

# PREPARING YOUR KITCHEN

Whenever I start a new housekeeping project or refresh my kitchen after stocks get low, I do a few things, starting with pulling everything out of the cupboards and discarding items that are old, expired, or have never been used. I also look at every food label on processed foods and get rid of anything that contains dairy and wipe down all the shelves with nontoxic cleaner to start fresh.

Simplicity is bliss and frees you to be more productive. Make time to grocery shop for pantry items that will accommodate your loved ones with dairy sensitivity, then fill those freshly cleaned shelves with the staple items detailed here, which include the items commonly used in this book.

## Stocking a Dairy-Free, Kid-Friendly Pantry

A well-stocked pantry is the key to dairy-free success. Cooking is much easier when you don't have to make a last-minute run to the store for a necessary ingredient. Also, keeping a supply of simple breakfast foods and on-the-go snacks makes life a lot simpler.

**Here is a list of some essential pantry items to get you started:**

**CANNED GOODS:** beans of all types; canned chicken, salmon, and tuna (all in water); corn; green and black olives; green beans; low-sodium beef broth, chicken broth, and vegetable broth; pumpkin puree; soups without dairy; tomato paste; tomato puree; vegetable mix

**CONDIMENTS:** apple cider vinegar, barbecue sauce, Dijon mustard, ketchup, mayonnaise, yellow mustard

**FLOURS AND BAKING ITEMS:** all-purpose flour (or gluten-free flour); baking powder; baking soda; cornstarch; dairy-free chocolate chips, chunks, and mini morsels; golden flaxseed meal; potato starch; tapioca flour; whole-wheat flour

**GRAINS AND PASTA:** assorted pasta noodles (macaroni, penne, spaghetti, etc.), long-grain white rice or brown rice, panko or dairy-free bread crumbs, quick-cooking oats and old-fashioned rolled oats

**MILKS:** canned coconut milk, cartons of plant-based milk, coconut cream

**NUTS AND SEEDS:** chia seeds, hemp seeds, nut butters, raw cashew nuts, salted nuts for snacking, unsalted whole and slivered almonds

**PROTEIN POWDER:** plain pea protein or plain vegan protein powder

**OILS:** avocado oil, coconut oil, cooking spray, olive oil

**SNACKS:** dried fruits such as blueberries, cranberries, and raisins

**SPICES AND DRIED HERBS:** dried basil, dried oregano, dried thyme, garlic powder, ground cinnamon, ground coriander, ground cumin, ground ginger, ground nutmeg, Italian seasoning, mild taco seasoning, nutritional yeast, onion powder, peppercorns, sea salt, turmeric

**SWEETENERS:** brown sugar, coconut sugar, honey, maple syrup, organic cane sugar

## Cooking with Common Dairy Substitutes

Traditional dairy plays a big role in cooking and is ubiquitous in baking. One big challenge for families switching to a dairy-free diet is how to find substitutions that do the work of dairy-based ingredients without sacrificing flavor and texture. The following recommendations will help you with common, easy-to-find substitutions.

**BUTTER:** I love using plant-based vegan butter because it tastes so similar to traditional butter. Use it in a 1:1 ratio where butter or ghee is called for, and when you need a fat that melts or spreads. Coconut oil in solid form can also be used 1:1 to replace butter in baking recipes. Virgin, or unrefined, coconut oil gives baked goods a pleasant mild coconut flavor, but if you prefer to avoid the coconut flavor, use refined coconut oil.

**CHEESE:** Cheese comes in so many forms: sliced, shredded, in sauces, and as spreads or dips. Luckily, there are tons of store-bought vegan options and they can be substituted 1:1 for dairy cheese. However, the flavor is somewhat different and some kids find it overpowering. I suggest weaning kids off milk-based cheese for a while before using a store-bought vegan version. In this book, I provide vegan cheese options for Homemade Shredding Cheese (page 174) as well as Queso Dipping Cheese (page 170), and Macaroni and Cheese with Peas (page 80). Nutritional yeast makes a great substitute for Parmesan cheese.

**CREAM:** Use canned coconut cream to replace dairy cream. It separates in the can, so make sure to shake the can first when using as a cream replacement or heat it to mix. If using it to make Whipped Cream (page 166), chill it for 24 hours first and do not mix or heat it before whipping. Use the solid cream in the can and save the water for another use, such as smoothies. Whip the solid cream in the same fashion you would heavy (whipping) cream.

**MILK:** Milk gives baked goods moisture and a fluffy texture. Replace dairy milk 1:1 with any plant-based milk in baking recipes and sauces.

**YOGURT:** Yogurt is wonderful to add to baked goods for moisture and bounce and to add creaminess to dressings, sauces, and soups. Use store-bought vegan yogurts 1:1 in baked goods, dressings, sauces, soups, and anything that calls for yogurt. Dairy-free yogurt is more liquid-y than other yogurts, so additional thickeners may be required for batters and sauces.

# PLANT-BASED MILKS

Plant-based milks are creamy, nutritious beverages that enable a dairy-free child to enjoy traditional food pairings and recipes, even a glass of milk with cookies! You may have to experiment to find the type your child likes best. There are many choices on the market, so if you don't have luck with one, don't lose heart.

**ALMOND MILK:** Wonderful in pancakes, baked goods, cereal, and oatmeal, almond milk can also be made into vegan ice cream.

**CASHEW MILK:** Cashew milk has a thicker consistency and is naturally sweet, which makes it fabulous for drinking and turning into a sweet drink with dates, vanilla, and cinnamon.

**COCONUT MILK:** Coconut milk comes in a variety of forms. Canned coconut milk, lite coconut milk, and coconut cream are used mostly in creamers, sauces, and for making ice cream. The boxed coconut beverage is wonderful for drinking or adding to smoothies, over cereals, and in baked goods.

**FLAX MILK:** Flaxseed is full of brain- and heart-healthy omega-3 fatty acids. Only a small amount of flaxseed is needed to blend and create this milk. Use it in baked goods, over oatmeal, and in smoothies.

**HEMP MILK:** This milk is loaded with iron and made from shelled hemp seeds. Use it in baked goods, cereals, and for smoothies.

**OAT MILK:** Oat milk is wonderfully creamy. Be careful not to heat or overblend it, as it can get sticky in texture. Strain the milk through a cloth flour sack for the best consistency. Use for baking, drinking, and smoothies.

**RICE MILK:** With a very thin consistency, rice milk is great for drinking and adding to hot and cold cereals.

# Equipment

When it comes to cooking at home, the tools you use will go a long way toward helping you achieve the results you desire. But that is not to say you need a lot of equipment, or that the equipment has to be fancy or expensive. There are a few must-have items—and a few more nice-to-have, but not essential, items—I recommend, which will help you cook with confidence, make recipes with ease, and create a finished dish your family loves.

## Must-Have

- Baking pans, including a 9-by-9-inch baking pan, a 9-by-13-inch baking pan, 2 rimmed sheet pans, and 2 (12-cup) muffin tins
- Cutting board
- Electric hand mixer
- High-speed blender
- Measuring tools, including a set of measuring cups, a set of measuring spoons, and a glass 2-cup liquid measuring cup

- Pots and pans, including a large nonstick skillet, stockpot, and a basic set of saucepans (small, medium, large) with lids
- Set of nested mixing bowls (small, medium, large)
- Sharp chef's knife
- Utensils, including an offset spatula (flipper), rubber spatula, whisk, and wooden spoon

## Nice to Have

- 24-cup mini muffin tin
- Food processor
- Immersion blender
- Rice cooker

- Slow cooker
- Spiralizer
- Stand mixer

# HOW THIS BOOK MAKES COOKING DAIRY-FREE FOR KIDS EASY

Kids can be picky eaters and most of us don't have time to deal with a lot of prep work or involved recipes, so I created recipes that use ingredients that are affordable, easy to find, and healthy—as well as perfect for kids' tastes. The recipes also don't require more than 45 minutes to 1 hour total prep and cooking time—unless it's cooked in the slow cooker or requires soaking or freezing—and half of them take 30 minutes or less to prepare. Each recipe also includes nutritional information, labels for dietary restrictions, and tips to simplify the recipe, substitute ingredients, or use leftovers. Each recipe was created with simplicity in mind so you can focus on the more important things in life.

One key to success is getting the kids involved. The moment kids start to experience solid foods, they form opinions on what they like and dislike. Share with them how the meal you create together will help their headaches go away, give them more energy, make their stomachs stop hurting, and help them feel much more comfortable overall. Have them stir vegan cheese sauces, boil noodles, and form nuggets with their own little hands. It builds an appreciation for the food and is more overpowering than the pain of a bellyache. If they complain, educate them about the benefits of the foods they're eating.

The recipes make it fun to eat as a family. Get creative with questions about what you want to dip your Chickpea Nuggets (page 76) in this time—will it be plain ketchup, "Special Sauce" (page 63), or Honey Mustard Sauce (168)? Or ask which ice-cream sundae toppings to try this week—marshmallows, mini chocolate chips, warm Caramel Sauce (page 167), homemade Whipped Cream (page 166), or maybe even all?

# 10 TIPS FOR PICKY EATERS

In many homes, dinnertime—or as we call it, "the mischief and chaos hour"—can be a battle that leaves you feeling defeated, powerless, and exhausted. These 10 tips will help you regain control and, hopefully, decrease "hangry" tantrums. It will also help your picky eater adapt to dairy-free foods while enjoying a balanced diet.

**1 Start slow.**
When you eliminate dishes that are cheesy or creamy, leave them out of the rotation for a while. That way, when you slowly reintroduce the vegan version, your child will be more likely to overlook any differences from what they may have enjoyed in the past.

**2 Don't allow heavy snacks before mealtime.**
Snacking too close to dinnertime fills kids up just enough to make dinner a battle and leave them hungry at bedtime.

**3 Set out freshly sliced vegetables as an appetizer.**
This is a great tip from my mom that I now do with my kids. Cut up broccoli, carrots, celery, colorful bell peppers, cucumbers, jicama, or any seasonal produce that tastes great raw. Vegetable appetizers keep kids just hungry enough to fuel up on the good stuff at dinner. Plus, when dinner is served, you don't have to worry about them eating their vegetables, because they already have.

**4 Make food fun!**
Roll out nuggets and cut them into shapes. Cut vegetables into shapes with cookie cutters. Make up fun names like "Hulk Nuggets." We always eat carrots for our "Superhero Super-Vision"!

**5** **Educate children on the health benefits of the foods they're eating.**
Kids are smart and being honest with them helps them understand and trust you. I tell my son the reasons we avoid cow's milk, and when he hears and understands those reasons, he doesn't fight me as much about the things he cannot eat.

**6** **Ask kids what they like.**
This is another great tip from my mom. There have been times when I have struggled opening a lunch box and seeing everything still in there! It drives me nuts because I hate wasting food. Mom said, "Then, ask him what *he* likes."

**7** **Give them A/B choices.**
Sometimes giving only two choices such as, "Do you want broccoli or kale leaves as your greens tonight?" gives kids a simple choice and makes them feel more in control. If they deny both, try my next suggestion.

**8** **Offer dessert.**
I know some parents don't agree with this one, but it works like a charm for us. If I know my kids need more food on a given day, I tell them they can have five small chocolate chips for dessert, or chocolate milk or ice cream or a cookie (if they eat all their dinner).

**9** **Keep trying.**
Kids' taste buds change and what they may not like one day, they will like the next. So, don't give up after the first try.

**10** **Let them make dinner!**
Designate a night where one child makes their favorite meal from this book (with your help, as needed).

*chapter two*

# PLANT-BASED MILKS

# OAT MILK

Oat milk is a rich and creamy blend of rolled oats and water strained into an earthy beverage. It does have an "oat-y" flavor and works best in baked goods, sauces, and soups. Oats are naturally gluten free, but they can have cross-contact with gluten during processing. If you want this oat milk to be gluten free, look for oats that specifically say "certified gluten free" on the packaging.

**PREP TIME:**
10 MINUTES

**MAKES
1 QUART**

1 cup old-fashioned rolled oats

4 cups filtered water

Pinch sea salt

¼ cup whole dates, pitted (optional)

1 teaspoon vanilla extract (optional)

1. In a high-speed blender, combine the oats, water, and salt. Blend on high speed for 30 to 60 seconds. Do not overblend.
2. Place a cloth flour sack, nut milk bag, or double layer of cheesecloth over a large bowl. Pour the blended mixture into the sack. Give the sack a good squeeze to push the milk into the bowl.
3. If you'd like to make this sweet, pour the strained milk back into the blender and add the dates and vanilla. Blend on high speed for 2 minutes, or until there are no visible date pieces.
4. Transfer the milk to a pitcher with a lid and refrigerate for up to 5 days.

**DID YOU KNOW?** If you soak, heat, or overblend oats, they can get gummy. That is what makes them creamy when eaten in oatmeal and what holds meat loaf together. When making plant milk with oats, make sure not to overblend the oats, only blending for 30 to 60 seconds.

# HEMP MILK

**ALLERGEN-FREE, EGG-FREE, GLUTEN-FREE, NUT-FREE, SOY-FREE, VEGAN**

Raw shelled hemp seeds are rich in omega-3s and omega-6s, and have more than 10 grams of protein per 3-tablespoon serving. This milk has a bit of a nutty flavor. Refrigerate any hemp seeds not used to make the milk and use them over cereal, sprinkled in salads, or added to smoothies.

**PREP TIME:**
10 MINUTES

**MAKES
1 QUART**

1⅓ cups shelled hemp seeds

4 cups filtered water

Pinch sea salt

¼ cup whole dates, pitted (optional)

1 teaspoon vanilla extract (optional)

1. In a high-speed blender, combine the hemp seeds, water, and salt. Blend on high speed for about 1 minute until well blended.
2. Place a cloth flour sack, nut milk bag, or double layer of cheesecloth over a large bowl. Pour the blended mixture into the bag. Give the sack a good squeeze to push the milk into the bowl.
3. If you'd like to make this sweet, pour the strained milk back into the blender and add the dates and vanilla. Blend on high speed for 2 minutes, or until there are no visible date pieces.
4. Transfer the milk to a pitcher with a lid and refrigerate for up to 5 days.

**SUBSTITUTION TIP:** If you don't have dates on hand, sweeten this milk, or any of the milks in this chapter, with 1 tablespoon maple syrup or honey (which will not be vegan) per 1 cup of milk.

# RICE MILK

This enjoyable drink comes together quickly. Rice milk is thinner than other alternative milk beverages and works well over cereal and oatmeal.

**PREP TIME:**
10 MINUTES

**MAKES 3 TO 4 CUPS**

1 cup raw long-grain white rice

4 cups filtered water

Pinch sea salt

¼ cup whole dates, pitted (optional)

1 teaspoon vanilla extract (optional)

**1.** In a high-speed blender, combine the rice, water, and salt. Blend on high speed for about 1 minute until well blended.

**2.** Place a cloth flour sack, nut milk bag, or double layer of cheesecloth over a large bowl. Pour the blended mixture into the bag. Give the bag a good squeeze to push the milk into the bowl.

**3.** If you'd like to make this sweet, pour the strained milk back into the blender and add the dates and vanilla. Blend on high speed for 2 minutes, or until there are no visible date pieces.

**4.** Transfer the milk to a pitcher with a lid and refrigerate for up to 5 days.

**SUBSTITUTION TIP:** Use 1 cup brown rice instead of white rice.

# FLAX MILK

Flax milk has become a satisfying new milk alternative in the past few years. It is superb added to smoothies and baked goods. Flaxseed is naturally rich in omega-3 fatty acids.

**PREP TIME:**
10 MINUTES,
PLUS 1 HOUR
TO REST

**MAKES
1 QUART**

¼ cup whole flaxseed

4 cups filtered water

Pinch sea salt

¼ cup whole dates, pitted (optional)

1 teaspoon vanilla extract (optional)

1. In a high-speed blender, combine the flaxseed, water, and salt. Blend on high speed for about 1 minute until well blended. Let rest for 30 to 60 minutes then remove the residue that floats on top.
2. Place a cloth flour sack, nut milk bag, or double layer of cheesecloth over a large bowl. Pour the blended mixture into the bag. Give the bag a good squeeze to push the milk into the bowl.
3. If you'd like to make this sweet, pour the strained milk back into the blender and add the dates and vanilla. Blend on high speed for 2 minutes, or until there are no visible date pieces.
4. Transfer the milk to a pitcher with a lid and refrigerate for up to 5 days.

**LEFTOVERS:** Any residue after straining can be saved and mixed in with baked goods, such as muffins, to add a nutrition boost.

# CASHEW MILK

This is one of my favorite plant-based milks to make. It is rich and creamy with a touch of natural sweetness. Cashew milk is used plain in sauces, smoothies, and soups, or alone as a sweetened beverage.

**PREP TIME:**
10 MINUTES,
PLUS 6 HOURS
TO SOAK

**MAKES
1 QUART**

1 cup raw
unsalted cashews

6 cups filtered
water, divided

Pinch sea salt

¼ cup whole dates,
pitted (optional)

1 teaspoon vanilla
extract (optional)

1. In a medium bowl, combine the cashews and 2 cups of filtered water. Refrigerate to soak for 6 hours. Drain and rinse the cashews under cold water.

2. In a high-speed blender, combine the drained cashews, remaining 4 cups of filtered water, and salt. Blend on high speed for about 1 minute, or until well blended.

3. Place a cloth flour sack, nut milk bag, or double layer of cheesecloth over a large bowl. Pour the blended mixture into the bag. Give the bag a good squeeze to push the milk into the bowl. Save the remaining cashew "meat" to add to muffins and baked goods.

4. If you'd like to make this sweet, pour the strained milk back into the blender and add the dates and vanilla. Blend on high speed for 2 minutes, or until there are no visible date pieces.

5. Transfer the milk to a pitcher with a lid and refrigerate for up to 5 days.

**SIMPLIFY IT:** To simplify the process, soak the cashews the night before. They can be soaked for up to 24 hours before using. Just be sure to rinse and drain them well to get any residue off the nuts.

# ALMOND MILK

One of the most popular milk alternatives is almond milk. You can find it in the cold section and on shelves, although most store-bought versions have extra ingredients to make the milk thicker. This almond milk is made from three simple ingredients, with an option for sweetening. The taste is heavenly and slightly creamy.

**PREP TIME:**
10 MINUTES,
PLUS 6 HOURS
TO SOAK

**MAKES
1 QUART**

1 cup unsalted raw almonds

6 cups filtered water, divided

Pinch sea salt

¼ cup whole dates, pitted (optional)

1 teaspoon vanilla extract (optional)

1. In a medium bowl, combine the almonds and 2 cups of filtered water. Refrigerate to soak for 6 hours. Drain and rinse the almonds under cold water.
2. In a high-speed blender, combine the drained almonds, remaining 4 cups of filtered water, and salt. Blend on high speed for about 1 minute, or until well blended.
3. Place a cloth flour sack, nut milk bag, or double layer of cheesecloth over a large bowl. Pour the blended mixture into the bag. Give the bag a good squeeze to push the milk into the bowl. Save the remaining almond "meat" to add to muffins and baked goods.
4. If you'd like to make this sweet, pour the strained milk back into the blender and add the dates and vanilla. Blend on high speed for 2 minutes, or until there are no visible date pieces.
5. Transfer the milk to a pitcher with a lid and refrigerate for up to 5 days.

**DID YOU KNOW?** With any plant-based milk, some settlement and separation will occur during refrigeration. It is best to shake the milk before serving.

*chapter three*

# BREAKFASTS AND SMOOTHIES

# MIXED BERRY SMOOTHIE

EGG-FREE, GLUTEN-FREE, VEGAN

I recommend keeping a small assortment of frozen fruits, including berries, sliced bananas, mango chunks, and pineapple chunks, on hand. Smoothies are a healthy snack that can be made any time of day. They squelch a "hangry" mood fast and kids love them. For a little extra fun, add a dollop of Whipped Cream (page 166) on top!

**PREP TIME:**
10 MINUTES

**MAKES
1 SMOOTHIE**

1½ cups frozen mixed berries

½ banana, sliced, frozen

½ cup apple juice

1 scoop plain vegan protein powder

1 tablespoon chia seeds

1 tablespoon hemp seeds

➔ In a high-speed blender, combine the berries, banana, apple juice, protein powder, chia seeds, and hemp seeds. Blend on high speed until smooth.

**MAKE IT YOUR OWN:** Use any of your favorite vegan protein blends or pea protein. Make sure to read the label on any protein powders to make sure there are no hidden dairy ingredients. The protein powder can also be left out, which makes the smoothie richer in berry flavor.

# TROPICAL PINEAPPLE-MANGO SMOOTHIE

EGG-FREE, GLUTEN-FREE, VEGAN

Anytime we go to the smoothie shop, my youngest orders a tropical pine-apple smoothie—except those smoothies are made with a scoop of frozen sweet milk. This version is perfect for the child that loves those smoothies but without the dairy. Protein powder provides extra nutrition, but you can always leave it out.

**PREP TIME:**
10 MINUTES

**MAKES
1 SMOOTHIE**

1 cup frozen pineapple chunks

½ cup frozen mango chunks

½ banana, sliced, frozen

1 scoop plain vegan protein powder

½ to ¾ cup pineapple juice

→ In a high-speed blender, combine the pineapple, mango, banana, protein powder, and ½ cup of pineapple juice. Blend on high speed until smooth. Add up to ¼ cup more pineapple juice, if needed, for texture.

**SUBSTITUTION TIP:** Don't have pineapple juice? Use coconut water instead.

# CHOCOLATE-PEANUT BUTTER SMOOTHIE

EGG-FREE, GLUTEN-FREE, VEGAN

This smoothie is a dairy-free version of a rich and creamy chocolate and peanut butter milkshake. It is naturally sweetened with dates, but you can also use 1 to 2 tablespoons maple syrup or honey instead.

**PREP TIME:**
10 MINUTES

**MAKES
1 SMOOTHIE**

1 cup dairy-free milk

2 tablespoons peanut butter

1 tablespoon cocoa powder

1 scoop plain vegan protein powder

2 whole dates, pitted

¼ teaspoon vanilla extract

½ to ¾ cup ice

➜ In a high-speed blender, combine the milk, peanut butter, cocoa powder, protein powder, dates, vanilla, and ½ cup of ice. Blend on high speed until smooth. Add ¼ cup more ice, if needed for texture.

**SUBSTITUTION TIP:** For kids with a peanut allergy, swap the peanut butter for a nut or seed butter that works for them.

# PEANUT BUTTER, HONEY, AND OAT BITES

**EGG-FREE, SOY-FREE, VEGETARIAN**

I started giving these to my kids for breakfast when they were toddlers. They could pick them up with their tiny hands and not make too much of a mess. Now, I make them and keep them on hand for an anytime meal or snack. I even serve them to my kids as dessert if they "eat all their dinner" and, sure enough, those plates are usually licked clean!

**PREP TIME:**
15 MINUTES

**MAKES 26 (1-INCH) BITES OR 13 (2-INCH) BITES**

1¼ cups quick-cooking oats

1 cup golden flax meal

½ cup almond butter or peanut butter

⅓ cup honey

2 tablespoons coconut oil, melted

1 tablespoon chia seeds

¼ teaspoon ground cinnamon

1 teaspoon vanilla extract

½ cup dairy-free and soy-free mini chocolate chips

1. Line a large storage container with parchment paper.
2. In a large bowl, combine the oats, flax meal, almond butter, honey, coconut oil, chia seeds, cinnamon, vanilla, and chocolate chips. Mix well.
3. Using clean hands, roll the dough into 1- or 2-inch balls and set them directly into the storage container. Cover and refrigerate for up to 5 days.

**TROUBLESHOOTING TIP:** If the dough is dry, add water, 1 tablespoon at a time, just until the dough pulls together. If the dough is too liquid, wrap it in plastic wrap and refrigerate for 30 minutes, then roll into balls. The oats will absorb the liquid.

# CINNAMON SPICE AND EVERYTHING NICE OATMEAL

We don't typically eat cereal; instead, my kids request oatmeal almost every morning. Specifically, they ask for lots of brown sugar, which is really coconut sugar in our home. Oatmeal, packed with fiber and iron, helps fuel kids for hours. These smooth oatmeal bowls are enriched with flax meal and hemp seeds, which blend into the color and consistency of oats while providing extra nutrition.

**PREP TIME:**
10 MINUTES

**COOK TIME:**
5 MINUTES

**SERVES 2**

2 cups water

1 cup quick-cooking oats

6 tablespoons hemp seeds

2 tablespoons golden flax meal

2 to 4 tablespoons coconut sugar or brown sugar

½ teaspoon ground cinnamon

¼ teaspoon ground nutmeg

Pinch sea salt

½ cup almond milk or cashew milk

Fresh fruit, nuts, seeds, or nut butter, for topping (optional)

1. In a medium saucepan over medium heat, bring the water to a boil. Add the oats. Cook for about 1 minute, stirring occasionally.
2. Turn off the heat and stir in the hemp seeds, flax meal, coconut sugar, cinnamon, nutmeg, salt, and up to ½ cup of almond milk. Mix well.

**3.** Serve with toppings such as banana slices, fresh fruit, nuts, and seed butter or nut butter, if desired.

**MAKE IT YOUR OWN:** You can also make this in the microwave. In a medium microwave-safe bowl, combine the water and oats. Microwave on high power for 1½ to 2 minutes, then proceed with steps 2 and 3 as directed.

# EVERYDAY OAT PANCAKES

**VEGETARIAN**

These pancakes are a simple way to get kids eating heart-healthy fiber and brain-boosting omega-3s first thing in the morning. But these pancakes aren't just for breakfast. You can use them as the bread for peanut butter and jelly sandwiches for lunches and snacks. They also freeze well, so double or triple the batter and store some cooked pancakes in a sealed freezer bag in the freezer, then thaw in the refrigerator the night before for a great grab-and-go breakfast on busy mornings.

**PREP TIME:**
15 MINUTES

**COOK TME:**
20 MINUTES

**MAKES ABOUT 15 SMALL PANCAKES (3 PER SERVING)**

Nonstick cooking spray

1 cup oat flour

½ cup potato starch

2½ teaspoons baking powder

¼ teaspoon sea salt

2 large eggs

1 cup dairy-free milk

2 tablespoons extra-virgin olive oil

1 tablespoon maple syrup

1 tablespoon distilled white vinegar

1 batch Whipped Cream (page 166)

**1.** Lightly coat a griddle with cooking spray. Heat the griddle over medium heat.

**2.** In a large bowl, whisk the flour, potato starch, baking powder, and salt to combine.

**3.** In a small bowl, whisk the eggs, milk, oil, maple syrup, and vinegar to blend.

4. Pour the wet ingredients into the dry ingredients and whisk just until combined. The batter may be slightly lumpy. Let stand for 5 minutes.

5. Reduce the heat under the griddle to medium-low. For each pancake drop a scant ¼ cup of batter onto the griddle (you should be able to cook 3 or 4 pancakes at a time, depending on the size of your griddle pan). Cook for 2 to 3 minutes, or until bubbles form. Flip and cook for 2 minutes more, or until golden brown. Repeat this process with the remaining batter.

6. Serve with whipped cream.

**SERVING SUGGESTION:** Let your kids get creative! Arrange a pancake bar with an assortment of fresh berries, banana slices, whipped cream, syrup, and nut butters for topping.

# BAKED CORNFLAKE-CRUSTED ORANGE JUICE FRENCH TOAST STICKS

When I was growing up, my mom was always making fresh homemade orange bread. The house smelled divine, especially when she turned that orange bread into French toast. This version uses dairy-free bread with fresh orange juice and zest for a twist on my favorite French toast. I like to bake it. That way you are not standing over the stove while everyone else eats—you can sit down, eat together, and enjoy your kids' giggles of delight!

**PREP TIME:**
15 MINUTES

**COOK TIME:**
15 MINUTES

**SERVES 9 (ABOUT 6 STICKS EACH)**

1 loaf dairy-free bread

6 large eggs

¾ cup dairy-free milk

½ cup freshly squeezed orange juice

1 teaspoon grated orange zest

1 teaspoon vanilla extract

1 teaspoon ground cinnamon

1½ cups crushed cornflakes

Confectioners' sugar, for serving (optional)

Maple syrup, for serving

1. Preheat the oven to 425°F. Line 2 baking sheets with parchment paper.
2. Cut each piece of bread into thirds and place the slices in an ungreased 9-by-13-inch baking dish.
3. In a large bowl, whisk the eggs, milk, orange juice, orange zest, vanilla, and cinnamon until well blended. Pour the batter over the bread and let soak for 2 minutes, turning once and making sure all the bread pieces are well coated.
4. One at a time, gently transfer the French toast sticks to the prepared baking sheets, allowing the extra liquid to drip off into the baking dish. Sprinkle each stick with cornflakes then flip and sprinkle cornflakes on the other side.

**5.** Bake for 6 minutes. Flip the French toast sticks and cook for 8 minutes more, or until golden brown.

**6.** Sprinkle with confectioners' sugar (if using) and serve with maple syrup.

**SUBSTITUTION TIP:** If you do not want the orange flavor, swap the orange juice for more milk and omit the orange zest.

# HEALTHY CARROT, AVOCADO, AND BANANA OAT MUFFINS

I love to add vegetables to baked goods. These healthy muffins are made with pureed carrot, avocado, banana, and oats for a nutrient-dense meal or snack kids love!

**PREP TIME:**
15 MINUTES

**COOK TIME:**
20 MINUTES,
PLUS
10 MINUTES
TO COOL

**MAKES
12 MUFFINS**

Nonstick cooking spray

1 cup whole-wheat flour

½ cup plus 2 tablespoons old-fashioned rolled oats

1½ teaspoons baking powder

1 teaspoon ground cinnamon

½ teaspoon baking soda

½ teaspoon sea salt

¼ teaspoon ground nutmeg

1 cup halved baby carrots

1 avocado, halved, pitted, and flesh scooped out

2 ripe bananas, mashed (about 1½ cups)

2 large eggs

½ cup maple syrup

1 teaspoon vanilla extract

1. Preheat the oven to 375°F. Lightly coat the interior of a 12-cup muffin tin with cooking spray, or line it with paper muffin cups.

2. In a large bowl, whisk the flour, oats, baking powder, cinnamon, baking soda, salt, and nutmeg to blend.

3. In a high-speed blender or food processor, combine the carrots, avocado flesh, mashed bananas, eggs, maple syrup, and vanilla. Blend until smooth.

4. Pour the wet ingredients into the dry ingredients and mix until incorporated. Evenly divide the batter among the prepared muffin cups.

5. Bake for 20 minutes, or until the tops begin to brown and a toothpick inserted into the center of a muffin comes out clean.

6. Let the muffins cool in the pan for about 10 minutes before turning them out onto a wire cooling rack.

**LEFTOVERS:** Leftovers are best when refrigerated in an airtight container for up to 3 days and reheated before consuming. Or, freeze leftover muffins in a sealed airtight freezer bag for up to 3 months.

# SAUSAGE AND POTATO BREAKFAST BURRITOS

With three hungry boys in the house, this is a go-to weekend breakfast. It is full of hearty, flavorful sausage, sautéed potatoes, and scrambled eggs. It keeps them going before games on weekends. This is an excellent protein-filled meal that can be ready at a moment's notice.

**PREP TIME:**
15 MINUTES

**COOK TIME:**
20 MINUTES

**MAKES
4 BURRITOS**

2 tablespoons olive oil, divided

2 large Yukon Gold potatoes, cut into ½-inch cubes

4 ounces turkey sausage

½ teaspoon ground cumin

6 large eggs

2 tablespoons dairy-free milk

¼ teaspoon sea salt

Freshly ground black pepper

4 (8-inch) flour tortillas

Fresh avocado slices (optional)

Salsa or organic ketchup, for topping (optional)

1. In a large skillet over medium-high heat, heat 1 tablespoon of oil. Add the potatoes and cook for 10 minutes, stirring regularly, or until cooked through. Transfer to a medium bowl and cover to keep warm.

2. Return the skillet to medium-high heat and add the sausage and cumin. Cook, breaking up the sausage as you stir, for 5 to 7 minutes, or until the sausage is cooked through and no pink remains. Add the sausage to the potatoes and re-cover.

3. In a large bowl, combine the eggs, milk, and salt and season with pepper to taste. Whisk for 30 seconds to blend.

4. In a medium skillet over medium-low heat, heat the remaining 1 tablespoon of oil. Pour in the eggs and let cook for 1 minute without stirring. With a wooden spoon or heat-proof rubber spatula, cook, stirring the eggs constantly, for

about 2 minutes more, or until fully cooked. Gently stir in the cooked potatoes and sausage.

5. Set out 4 plates. Place 1 tortilla on each plate. Put an equal amount of sausage and egg mixture in the center of each tortilla. Add avocado slices (if using). For each burrito, fold in the sides toward the middle then, starting at the end closest to you, roll up the burrito. Serve topped with salsa or ketchup (if using).

**LEFTOVERS:** Serve leftover burritos another morning, or for lunch or dinner. They will last, covered and refrigerated, for 1 day with avocado and for 3 days without. Wrap individually in parchment paper, then wrap in foil. Seal tightly. Reheat on a baking sheet, covered with foil, in a 350°F oven for 15 minutes, or until warm. You can also microwave them on high power for about 1 minute.

*chapter four*

# SOUPS AND SALADS

# MINESTRONE ALPHABET SOUP

This soup bursts with savory flavors and loads of vegetables that kids enjoy. The leftovers are even better, as the flavors have time to settle and blend.

**PREP TIME:**
15 MINUTES

**COOK TIME:**
40 MINUTES

**SERVES 4**

2 tablespoons olive oil

1 cup chopped white onion

½ cup chopped carrot

½ cup diced celery

2 garlic cloves, minced

1 (15-ounce) can white cannellini beans, drained and rinsed

4 cups low-sodium vegetable broth

1 (14.5-ounce) can fire-roasted diced tomatoes with green chilies

1 zucchini, diced

1½ tablespoons Italian seasoning

1 bay leaf

1 tablespoon nutritional yeast

½ teaspoon sea salt, plus more for seasoning

½ teaspoon freshly ground black pepper, plus more for seasoning

1 cup chopped fresh spinach

2 cups cooked alphabet pasta

Fresh parsley, for garnish

**1.** In a large pot over medium heat, heat the oil. Add the onion, carrot, celery, and garlic. Sauté for about 5 minutes until tender and fragrant.

**2.** Add the white beans, vegetable broth, tomatoes and green chilies, zucchini, Italian seasoning, bay leaf, nutritional yeast, salt, and pepper. Cover the pot and reduce the heat to low. Cook for 30 minutes.

**3.** Add the spinach, re-cover the pot, and cook for about 1 minute until the spinach wilts.

4. Remove and discard the bay leaf. Taste the soup and season with salt and pepper, if needed.
5. Stir in the cooked pasta right before serving and garnish with parsley.

**SUBSTITUTION TIP:** Alphabet pasta makes it fun for kids, but if you don't have any on hand, star-shaped pasta, small shells, or macaroni also works well. To make this soup gluten free, omit the pasta or use a gluten-free variety.

# TOMATO-BASIL SOUP

This scrumptious soup is my kids' absolute favorite. Try this in summer when tomatoes are at their ripest and basil is plentiful. Serve warm with a vegan grilled cheese sandwich and the crowd will go wild!

**PREP TIME:**
10 MINUTES

**COOK TIME:**
35 MINUTES

**SERVES 4**

2 pounds Roma, vine, or grape tomatoes, halved

2 cups low-sodium vegetable broth

1 large carrot, chopped

½ cup chopped sweet onion

4 garlic cloves, minced

2 tablespoons extra-virgin olive oil

½ cup fresh basil leaves, plus more for garnish

1½ teaspoons sea salt

¼ teaspoon freshly ground black pepper

**1.** In a large saucepan over medium-high heat, combine the tomatoes, vegetable broth, carrot, onion, garlic, oil, basil, salt, and pepper. Cover the pan and bring the soup to a boil. Reduce the heat to low and simmer the soup for 30 minutes.

**2.** Remove the pan from the heat. Using an immersion blender, or carefully transferring the soup to a standard blender and adding the lid (making sure to vent to allow steam to escape), puree the soup to your desired thickness. If needed, return the soup to the heat to rewarm before serving. Garnish with fresh basil.

**SIMPLIFY IT:** Replace the fresh tomatoes with 2 (14.5-ounce) cans fire-roasted tomatoes and enjoy this soup year-round!

# BUTTERNUT SQUASH SOUP

**EGG-FREE, GLUTEN-FREE, SOY-FREE, VEGAN**

Kids love creamy soups and this one boasts naturally sweet flavors. Using frozen squash chunks means that this velvety dish can be made and on the table in under an hour. This simple meal is terrific served with crackers for the kids to dip into their soup.

**PREP TIME:**
15 MINUTES

**COOK TIME:**
30 MINUTES

**SERVES 4**

2 tablespoons olive oil

1 small yellow onion, chopped

½ cup chopped carrot

½ cup chopped celery

4 garlic cloves, minced

2 (12-ounce) bags frozen butternut squash chunks

4 cups low-sodium vegetable broth

1 tablespoon nutritional yeast

½ teaspoon sea salt

½ teaspoon freshly ground black pepper

⅓ cup plain coconut-milk yogurt

1. In a large saucepan over medium-high heat, heat the oil. Add the onion, carrot, celery, garlic, and squash. Cook for about 15 minutes, stirring often, until the vegetables are tender.
2. Add the vegetable broth, nutritional yeast, salt, and pepper. Reduce the heat to low and simmer the soup for 10 minutes to let the flavors combine.
3. Remove from the heat. Using an immersion blender, or carefully transferring the soup to a standard blender and adding the lid (making sure to vent to allow steam to escape), puree the soup for about 2 minutes until smooth.
4. Stir in the yogurt right before serving.

# MOM'S CHICKEN NOODLE SOUP

**NUT-FREE, SOY-FREE**

There is nothing better than Mom's chicken noodle soup when kids are feeling under the weather. Making this soup is a special way to nurture your children when they need an extra dose of comfort. This version is a blend of clear broth, succulent chicken, light vegetables, and egg noodles that will warm the body and soothe the spirit.

**PREP TIME:**
15 MINUTES

**COOK TIME:**
45 MINUTES

**SERVES 8**

4 cups low-sodium chicken broth

2 cups water

1½ pounds bone-in, skin-on chicken thighs

3 cups chopped carrot

1 cup chopped celery

1 yellow onion, chopped

6 ounces egg noodles

1 cup fresh parsley, chopped

2 tablespoons fresh thyme leaves, or ½ teaspoon dried thyme

1. In a large stockpot over high heat, combine the chicken broth, water, chicken thighs, carrot, celery, and onion. Cover the pot and bring to a boil. Once boiling, reduce the heat to low. Continue to cook the soup, covered, for 25 minutes more, or until the chicken is cooked through.

2. Using a slotted spoon, transfer the chicken to a cutting board. When cool enough to handle, use a fork to separate the meat from the skin and bones. Put the meat back into the pot and discard the skin and bones.

3. Increase the heat to medium-high and bring the soup to a boil. Add the noodles and cook for 7 to 10 minutes, or until tender.

4. Add the parsley and thyme just before serving.

**LEFTOVERS:** Don't be shy of leftovers. This soup is also incredible the day after cooking, when the flavors have blended and the soup thickens.

# LENTIL AND BACON SOUP

**EGG-FREE, GLUTEN-FREE**

When we visit my mom in Virginia, she loves to make my kids lentil soup. To my surprise, the first time they had it they loved it! Hers is a thick soup made of lentils, onion, celery, and carrot with a ham bone for flavoring. For this version, I like to use bacon bits for a smoky, salty flavor.

**PREP TIME:**
10 MINUTES

**COOK TIME:**
50 MINUTES

**SERVES 6**

1 tablespoon coconut oil

1 large yellow onion, chopped

1 cup chopped carrot

½ cup chopped celery

2 garlic cloves, minced

1 teaspoon ground coriander

½ teaspoon ground cinnamon

¾ teaspoon sea salt

1 cup dried lentils, picked over for debris

1 (14-ounce) can fire-roasted tomatoes, with their juices

4 cups water

¾ cup bacon bits

⅓ cup plain coconut-milk yogurt

1. In a large saucepan over medium heat, heat the oil. Add the onion, carrot, celery, garlic, coriander, cinnamon, and salt. Cook for 5 minutes, or until the onion is slightly translucent.
2. Add the lentils, tomatoes with their juices, and water. Bring the soup to a boil. Once boiling, reduce the heat to low, stir in the bacon bits, and simmer the soup for 40 minutes, or until the lentils are tender.
3. Stir in the yogurt right before serving.

**SUBSTITUTION TIP:** Use crumbled pieces of sliced bacon rather than bacon bits for a rich alternative.

# CILANTRO-LIME SHREDDED CABBAGE SLAW

ALLERGEN-FREE, EGG-FREE, GLUTEN-FREE, NUT-FREE, SOY-FREE, VEGAN

This zesty, crunchy, colorful salad is a favorite of my youngest, who requests it often as a side. It also makes a refreshing topping for tacos, nachos, burgers, and salad.

**PREP TIME:**
20 MINUTES

**SERVES 4**

2 tablespoons apple cider vinegar

2 tablespoons olive oil

2 tablespoons freshly squeezed lime juice

1 tablespoon organic cane sugar

¼ teaspoon sea salt

8 ounces shredded cabbage

5 radishes, cut into very thin slivers or shredded

⅓ cup finely chopped red bell pepper

⅓ cup chopped fresh cilantro

1 carrot, shredded

1. In a large bowl, whisk the vinegar, oil, lime juice, sugar, and salt to blend.
2. Add the cabbage, radishes, red bell pepper, cilantro, and carrot. Toss well to combine and coat. Serve immediately.

**MAKE IT YOUR OWN:** Switch up the flavors and colors of this slaw using a combination of green and red cabbage, add apples cut into small cubes for sweetness, or add about ¼ teaspoon ground cumin to the dressing.

# EGG SALAD AVOCADO BOATS

**GLUTEN-FREE, NUT-FREE, SOY-FREE, VEGETARIAN**

This version of egg salad is not served on boring old sandwich bread but piled on top of half a creamy avocado. Finely diced red pepper and celery boost the flavor and nutritional value. Kids and parents alike will love this twist on the lunchtime classic.

**PREP TIME:**
20 MINUTES

**SERVES 4**

4 hard-boiled eggs, peeled and diced

½ cup finely diced celery

½ red bell pepper, finely diced

⅓ cup mayonnaise

1 tablespoon chopped fresh cilantro leaves, plus more for garnish

1 tablespoon yellow mustard

2 teaspoons freshly squeezed lemon juice

¼ teaspoon sea salt

¼ teaspoon ground white pepper

2 large avocados, halved and pitted

1. In a medium bowl, combine the eggs, celery, red bell pepper, mayonnaise, cilantro, mustard, lemon juice, salt, and pepper. Gently stir to coat.
2. Evenly divide the egg mixture into the avocado halves and serve with a spoon.

**SERVING SUGGESTION:** Instead of making the avocados into boats, mash the avocado into the egg salad or serve it on the side, cut into slices or diced.

# TANGY CORN, TOMATO, AND CHICKPEA SALAD

**ALLERGEN-FREE, EGG-FREE, GLUTEN-FREE, NUT-FREE, SOY-FREE, VEGAN**

This simple salad takes no time at all to prepare and is something everyone in the family will love. It has a touch of sweetness from the corn and tomatoes, and the chickpeas add protein for a flavorful plant-based meal.

**PREP TIME:**
10 MINUTES

**SERVES 4**

### FOR THE SALAD
1 (16-ounce) bag frozen corn, thawed

1 (15-ounce) can chickpeas, drained and rinsed

1 cup halved grape tomatoes

⅓ cup diced scallion, green and white parts

Sea salt

Freshly ground black pepper

### FOR THE DRESSING
1 teaspoon Dijon mustard

2 tablespoons apple cider vinegar

¼ cup olive oil

### TO MAKE THE SALAD
1. In a large bowl, combine the corn, chickpeas, tomatoes, and scallion. Season with salt and pepper to taste.

### TO MAKE THE DRESSING
2. In a small bowl, whisk the mustard and vinegar to blend. Add the olive oil and whisk until combined.
3. Pour the dressing over the salad right before you are ready to serve and gently stir to coat. Serve at room temperature or slightly chilled.

**SERVING SUGGESTION:** Serve this for lunch or as a side dish. For a heartier meal, serve it atop chopped kale with Tortilla-Crusted Chicken Tenders (page 110).

# COWBOY CAVIAR SALAD

ALLERGEN-FREE, EGG-FREE, GLUTEN-FREE, NUT-FREE, SOY-FREE, VEGAN

A colorful healthy dish made of beans, corn, vegetables, and black-eyed peas. If you serve this simple salad as a main dish for lunch or dinner, rest assured your family is getting ample nutrition. This powerhouse is loaded with protein, vitamin C, and fiber!

**PREP TIME:**
15 MINUTES

**SERVES 4**

1 red bell pepper, finely chopped

1 Roma tomato, finely chopped

1 (15-ounce) can black beans, drained and rinsed

1 (15-ounce) can black-eyed peas, drained and rinsed

2 cups frozen corn, thawed

⅓ cup finely chopped green bell pepper

¼ cup chopped fresh cilantro

1 tablespoon extra-virgin olive oil

Juice of 1 lime

Grated zest of 1 lime

¼ teaspoon sea salt

¼ teaspoon freshly ground black pepper

→ In a large bowl, toss together the red bell pepper, tomato, black beans, black-eyed peas, corn, green bell pepper, cilantro, oil, lime juice, lime zest, salt, and pepper. Serve.

**SERVING SUGGESTION:** Serve this as a dip with chips, over chips as nachos topped with vegan cheese, or as a filling in a burrito with store-bought vegan cheese, or Homemade Shredding Cheese (page 174).

# CHILLED TACO SALAD WITH PASTA

Finger foods are my favorite for toddlers and young children, and this taco salad is great for tiny fingers. Little ones will find tender morsels of all their favorites, including pasta, avocado, beans, and tomatoes. But don't get me wrong, this mouthwatering, yet mild, taco salad isn't *only* for the youngest members of the family. Those who have graduated to forks and knives will love it, too!

**PREP TIME:**
15 MINUTES

**COOK TIME:**
10 MINUTES

**SERVES 4**

1 cup dried macaroni

1 (15-ounce) can black beans, drained and rinsed

1 (4-ounce) can diced green chilies

1 cup corn, fresh or frozen (and thawed)

1 large avocado, peeled, halved, pitted, and chopped

¼ cup chopped fresh cilantro

3 Roma tomatoes, diced

1 (1.4-ounce) packet mild taco seasoning mix

2 tablespoons freshly squeezed lime juice

2 tablespoons olive oil

½ cup shredded vegan cheese or Homemade Shredding Cheese (page 174), for topping (optional)

1. Fill a medium stockpot two-thirds full of water and bring it to a boil over high heat. Pour in the macaroni and cook for 5 to 7 minutes, or until tender. Drain.
2. In a large bowl, combine the cooked macaroni, black beans, green chilies, corn, avocado, cilantro, and tomatoes.
3. In a small bowl, whisk the taco seasoning, lime juice, and oil to blend. Pour the dressing over the salad and toss to coat. Top with shredded cheese (if using).

**LEFTOVERS:** Leftovers can be used as a filling for a wrap. Put a little salad inside a flour tortilla (you can also add leftover chicken, if you have it), and roll it up for a quick leftovers lunch.

# BAKED CINNAMON APPLES

**EGG-FREE, NUT-FREE, VEGAN**

These mouthwatering apples are baked in butter, sugar, and cinnamon. When I was a kid, my mom would serve cinnamon applesauce as a side with dinner. I think these are almost better.

**PREP TIME:**
20 MINUTES

**COOK TIME:**
25 MINUTES

**SERVES 6**

Nonstick cooking spray

5 apples, peeled, cored, and diced

½ cup organic cane sugar

2 teaspoons all-purpose flour

2 teaspoons ground cinnamon

¼ teaspoon ground nutmeg

6 tablespoons (¾ stick) vegan butter

1. Preheat the oven to 350°F. Lightly coat a 9-by-9-inch baking pan with cooking spray.

2. In a large bowl, toss together the apples, sugar, flour, cinnamon, and nutmeg to coat. Transfer the apples to the prepared baking dish. Evenly drop tablespoons of butter on top of the apples.

3. Bake for 25 minutes until the apples are tender. Serve as a side, snack, or dessert with a scoop of dairy-free ice cream.

**MAKE IT YOUR OWN:** If your children prefer applesauce, simply put the cooked apples in a food processor or blender and puree. You can also change up the recipe using pears in place of apples.

# CRISPY SAUTÉED GREEN BEANS

What's not to love about tender green beans tossed in a light, bright lemon-Dijon dressing? This is a wonderful recipe to serve as a side with Tortilla-Crusted Chicken Tenders (page 110) or Cod Baked in Parchment (page 94).

**PREP TIME:**
15 MINUTES

**COOK TIME:**
6 MINUTES

**SERVES 4**

2 tablespoons olive oil, divided

1 tablespoon freshly squeezed lemon juice

1 teaspoon Dijon mustard

½ teaspoon sea salt

¼ teaspoon freshly ground black pepper

1 pound green beans, trimmed on both ends

1. In a small bowl, whisk 1 tablespoon of oil, the lemon juice, Dijon, salt, and pepper until combined.

2. In a large skillet over medium-high heat, heat the remaining 1 tablespoon of oil. Add the green beans and cook for 5 minutes, stirring constantly, or until the beans are a rich green color.

3. Turn off the heat, pour in the dressing, and toss to coat. Serve warm.

**LEFTOVERS:** Save any leftovers and use them in Minestrone Alphabet Soup (page 42) or Italian Tuna Casserole (page 100).

# ZUCCHINI FRIES

SOY-FREE, VEGETARIAN

I love finding fun ways to incorporate vegetables into kids' meals. These breaded zucchini fries are the perfect way to do just that. They have a crispy coating with a Parmesan cheese flavor, which is achieved using a blend of almond meal and nutritional yeast. Enjoy them dipped in Creamy Avocado Dressing (page 169) or Honey Mustard Sauce (page 168).

**PREP TIME:**
10 MINUTES, PLUS 20 MINUTES TO REST

**COOK TIME:**
20 MINUTES

**SERVES 4**

Nonstick cooking spray

1 large zucchini

½ teaspoon sea salt, plus more for preparing the zucchini

1 cup all-purpose flour

3 large eggs

1 cup panko bread crumbs

¾ cup almond meal

¼ cup nutritional yeast

1 tablespoon Italian seasoning

¼ teaspoon garlic powder

1 tablespoon chopped fresh parsley

1. Lightly coat a baking sheet with cooking spray.
2. Cut off the ends from the zucchini. Halve the zucchini lengthwise, then cut the zucchini into long slices by cutting each half into thirds lengthwise (if it is a very large zucchini cut it into fourths). Lay the zucchini slices on the prepared baking sheet and sprinkle with salt. Let sit for 20 minutes, then dab the water from the zucchini using paper towels.
3. Preheat the oven to 400°F. Fit a wire cooling rack over a baking sheet.
4. Set up a breading station with three small bowls. Put the flour into the first bowl. In the second bowl, whisk the eggs until they are well combined and a little frothy. In the third bowl, stir together the panko, almond meal, nutritional yeast, Italian seasoning, salt, and garlic powder.
5. Dip and thoroughly coat each zucchini slice in the flour, then the egg, and finally the breading. Set the breaded zucchini slices on the wire rack in a single layer.

6. Bake the zucchini strips for 10 minutes. Flip and bake the other side for 10 minutes more, or until golden brown.
7. Sprinkle with parsley and serve immediately.

**SUBSTITUTION TIP:** If your child has a nut allergy, omit the almond meal and replace it with 1 cup panko (totaling 2 cups for the recipe).

# GLAZED CARROTS

EGG-FREE, GLUTEN-FREE, NUT-FREE, VEGAN

Comforting fall spices, sweet maple syrup, and a creamy butter essence surround these carrots. I don't think I have ever seen a child turn down a sweet treat and these carrots taste like buttery sweet bliss.

**PREP TIME:**
15 MINUTES

**COOK TIME:**
25 MINUTES

**SERVES 4**

1 pound carrots, sliced diagonally into ½-inch pieces

3 tablespoons maple syrup

½ teaspoon ground cinnamon

¼ teaspoon sea salt

2 tablespoons vegan butter, melted

1. Preheat the oven to 425°F. Line a baking sheet with parchment paper.
2. Put the carrots on the prepared baking sheet.
3. In a small bowl, stir together the maple syrup, cinnamon, and salt. Pour the glaze over the carrots evenly, then pour the melted butter over the carrots in the same manner. Using your clean hands, toss to coat the carrots in the maple syrup, butter, and spices. Spread the carrots into an even layer on the baking sheet.
4. Bake the carrots for 10 minutes. Flip the carrots and bake for 10 to 15 minutes more until soft and glazed. Serve warm.

**SERVING SUGGESTION:** These are wonderful as a side with meat dishes, Crispy Breaded Fish Sticks (page 93), or Chickpea Nuggets (page 76).

# BROCCOLI TOTS

VEGETARIAN

This fun twist on tater tots uses broccoli as the base instead of potato and includes nutritional yeast for a Parmesan-like flavor. With an incredibly satisfying taste and a crispy texture kids love, no one will miss traditional tater tots.

**PREP TIME:**
15 MINUTES

**COOK TIME:**
40 MINUTES

**MAKES
36 TOTS
(9 PER
SERVING)**

3 cups broccoli florets, fresh or frozen

1 large egg

2 tablespoons grated onion

¾ cup dairy-free milk

1 cup panko bread crumbs

¼ cup nutritional yeast

1 tablespoon chopped fresh basil

½ teaspoon dried oregano

½ teaspoon sea salt

¼ teaspoon freshly ground black pepper

1. Preheat the oven to 400°F. Fit a wire cooling rack over a baking sheet.
2. Put 1 inch of water in the bottom of a large saucepan and fit it with a steamer basket. Bring the water to a boil over medium-high heat. Put the broccoli florets in the steamer basket, cover the pan, and steam the broccoli for 3 to 5 minutes, or until just tender. Transfer the broccoli to a cutting board and finely chop.
3. In a large bowl, combine the chopped broccoli, egg, onion, milk, panko, nutritional yeast, basil, oregano, salt, and pepper. Mix well to form a dough.
4. Using a tablespoon, scoop the mixture into your clean hands and form it into a 1-inch tater tot shape. Place each tot on the wire rack.
5. Bake for 15 minutes, turn the tots, and bake for 15 minutes more until slightly browned. Serve immediately.

**SUPPLEMENT TIP:** If your kids are picky about onion, substitute ½ teaspoon onion powder for the minced onion, or skip the onion altogether.

# CREAMY MASHED CAULIFLOWER

**EGG-FREE, GLUTEN-FREE, VEGAN**

For a change from traditional mashed potatoes, try this rich mashed cauliflower. This garlicky side is made with coconut milk for a creamy consistency. It is great with Mini Turkey Meatballs with Steamed Broccoli (page 116).

**PREP TIME:**
20 MINUTES

**COOK TIME:**
10 MINUTES

**SERVES 4**

1 large head cauliflower

2 garlic cloves, minced

3 tablespoons vegan butter

2 tablespoons coconut milk or coconut cream, plus more as needed

2 tablespoons potato starch

¾ teaspoon sea salt

¼ teaspoon ground white pepper

Chopped fresh chives, for garnish

1. Break the cauliflower into chunks and, in batches, put it into a food processor and process until smooth.
2. Transfer the pureed cauliflower to a microwaveable bowl and heat it in the microwave on high power for 5 minutes. Remove and let cool.
3. Meanwhile, in a small saucepan over medium-low heat, warm the garlic and butter for 3 to 5 minutes until the garlic is fragrant and the butter is melted. Put the garlic butter into the food processor.
4. Secure a nut bag or a doubled layer of cheesecloth over a medium bowl. Pour the cauliflower into the nut bag and squeeze to drain out all the liquid. Discard the liquid.
5. Place the drained cauliflower in the food processor. Add the coconut milk, potato starch, salt, and white pepper. Blend until smooth. For a thinner consistency, add more coconut milk, 1 teaspoon at a time. Serve warm garnished with chives.

**DID YOU KNOW?** Squeeze out as much water from the cauliflower as possible so you have a "potato" consistency to work with and for maximum flavor.

# BAKED POTATO WEDGES WITH "SPECIAL SAUCE"

**ALLERGEN-FREE, EGG-FREE, GLUTEN-FREE, NUT-FREE, SOY-FREE, VEGAN**

Crispy on the outside, tender on the inside! These thick homemade potato wedges are a tantalizing comfort food kids gravitate to. (You may want to double or triple the recipe to have extra on hand for the week!) Whenever we serve these, my boys eat them first—one dips his in this special sauce (created by him!) and the other eats them plain.

**PREP TIME:**
10 MINUTES

**COOK TIME:**
20 MINUTES

**SERVES 4**

**FOR THE POTATOES**

Nonstick cooking spray

2 large russet potatoes

3 tablespoons avocado oil

½ teaspoon sea salt

½ teaspoon freshly ground black pepper

**FOR THE SAUCE**

¼ cup organic ketchup

2 tablespoons yellow mustard

**TO MAKE THE POTATOES**

1. Preheat the oven to 400°F. Lightly coat a baking sheet with cooking spray.
2. Halve the potatoes lengthwise and cut each half lengthwise into 6 wedges. Place the potatoes in a large bowl and add the oil, salt, and pepper. Toss to coat. Arrange the wedges on the baking sheet in a single layer.
3. Bake for 10 minutes, turn the wedges, and bake for 10 minutes more until crisp on both sides.

**TO MAKE THE SAUCE**

4. Place the ketchup and mustard in small ramekins for kids to customize and use for dipping.

# CHILI MAC 'N' CHEESE BITES

My kids swoon over these little muffins. They are great to serve as a snack and they make a tasty meal with a side of steamed broccoli or Glazed Carrots (page 60). The recipe uses my Black Bean and Sweet Potato Chili (page 84), because we always have leftover chili, but any homemade or store-bought chili can be used.

**PREP TIME:**
35 MINUTES

**COOK TIME:**
35 MINUTES

**MAKES
24 MUFFIN
BITES (4 PER
SERVING)**

Nonstick cooking spray

1½ cups dried macaroni

1 cup panko bread crumbs, divided

2 tablespoons vegan butter

2 tablespoons all-purpose flour

½ teaspoon onion powder

½ teaspoon garlic powder

½ teaspoon salt

1 cup dairy-free milk

½ cup shredded vegan cheese

1 tablespoon nutritional yeast

2 large eggs, beaten

1 cup Black Bean and Sweet Potato Chili (page 84) or canned vegetarian chili

1. Preheat the oven to 425°F. Lightly coat the inside of 2 (12-cup) muffin tins with cooking spray.
2. Fill a large stockpot two-thirds full of water. Bring the water to a boil over high heat. Pour in the macaroni and cook for 5 to 7 minutes, or until tender. Drain.
3. Meanwhile, sprinkle ½ teaspoon of panko into the bottom of each prepared muffin cup.
4. In a large saucepan over medium heat, melt the butter. Add the flour, onion powder, garlic powder, and salt. Whisk to make a roux. Cook for about 7 minutes, stirring continuously, until thick. In a slow, steady stream, pour in the milk, whisking constantly. Bring the sauce to a simmer and cook, stirring, for 1 to 2 minutes, or until thickened. Add the shredded cheese and nutritional yeast. Whisk until the cheese melts.

**5.** Turn off the heat and add the eggs and ½ cup of panko, mixing so the eggs do not clump.

**6.** Add the chili and cooked macaroni and toss to coat. Spoon about 2 tablespoons of the mixture into each prepared muffin cup. Top each chili mac 'n' cheese bite with ½ teaspoon of the remaining panko.

**7.** Bake for 12 to 15 minutes, or until golden brown. Let cool in the pan for 5 minutes before serving.

**SIMPLIFY IT:** To make this meal easier, make the chili the night before and reserve 1 cup for this recipe.

# SIMPLE ROASTED VEGETABLES

When we need a quick vegetable fix on the table ASAP, roasted vegetables are always my go-to choice. I can pile all our favorite vegetables onto one sheet pan and bake them while making the main dish. This recipe is so simple and mildly flavored with oil, salt, onion, and garlic.

**PREP TIME:**
15 MINUTES

**COOK TIME:**
45 MINUTES

**SERVES 4**

4 large red potatoes, cut into ½-inch cubes

4 large carrots, cut into ½-inch-thick coins

2 cups trimmed and quartered Brussels sprouts

1½ tablespoons olive oil

1 teaspoon sea salt

½ teaspoon onion powder

½ teaspoon garlic powder

1. Preheat the oven to 400°F.
2. In a large bowl, combine the potatoes, carrots, and Brussels sprouts.
3. In a small bowl, whisk the oil, salt, onion powder, and garlic powder to combine. Pour the oil mixture over the vegetables and, using your clean hands, toss to coat. Spread the vegetables on a baking sheet in a single layer.
4. Bake for 25 minutes, flip the vegetables, and bake for 15 to 20 minutes more, or until slightly browned and soft.

**SUBSTITUTION TIP:** If your family loves sweet potatoes and butternut squash, swap out the potatoes and try either of those vegetables in its place. As a parent, it is all about offering foods over and over again and testing what kids like.

# HEALTHY PUMPKIN MUFFINS

## SOY-FREE, VEGETARIAN

Pumpkin is not just for fall and winter months. This recipe is on repeat at our house year-round. My kids love to have a muffin warmed in the microwave (about 15 seconds), halved, and with a bit of vegan butter spread on each side. It is one of the most delicious treats to serve for breakfast or as a quick snack on the go.

**PREP TIME:**
10 MINUTES

**COOK TIME:**
35 MINUTES

**MAKES
12 MUFFINS**

Nonstick cooking spray

1 (15-ounce) can pure pumpkin puree

3 large eggs

½ cup unsweetened applesauce

1½ teaspoons vanilla extract

1¾ cups whole-wheat flour

1 cup coconut sugar or packed light brown sugar

2 teaspoons baking powder

1 teaspoon ground cinnamon

½ teaspoon baking soda

¼ teaspoon sea salt

1. Preheat the oven to 350°F. Lightly coat the inside of a 12-cup muffin tin with cooking spray, or line it with paper muffin cups.
2. In a medium bowl, whisk the pumpkin, eggs, applesauce, and vanilla to blend.
3. In a large bowl, stir together the flour, coconut sugar, baking powder, cinnamon, baking soda, and salt. Make a well in the center of the dry ingredients. Pour the wet ingredients into the well in the dry ingredients and mix to combine. Evenly distribute the batter among the prepared muffin cups.
4. Bake for 28 to 33 minutes, or until the muffins start to brown on top and a toothpick inserted into the center of a muffin comes out clean.
5. Store in an airtight container for 2 to 3 days.

*chapter six*

# VEGETARIAN AND VEGAN MAINS

# CREAM CHEESE, SPINACH, AND CUCUMBER PINWHEELS

**EGG-FREE, VEGAN**

Pinwheel sandwiches are such a fun alternative to regular sandwiches. The one vegetable my kids always love year-round is cucumber, so I put it in everything I can.

**PREP TIME:**
15 MINUTES

**SERVES 4**

4 (10-inch) flour tortillas

8 tablespoons vegan cream cheese spread, plus more as needed

1 cup fresh baby spinach

1 English cucumber, peeled and thinly sliced

1. Lay the tortillas on a work surface. Evenly spread 2 tablespoons of cream cheese over each tortilla.
2. Add ¼ cup spinach to each tortilla in an even layer. Distribute the cucumber evenly among the tortillas.
3. Starting from the edge of one tortilla, roll it up tightly and seal the edges with cream cheese. Repeat with the remaining tortillas.
4. Cut each filled and rolled tortilla into 2-inch pieces. Serve immediately.

**MAKE IT YOUR OWN:** If your kids are adventurous eaters, add fresh herbs to these pinwheels. Basil, dill, mint, oregano, or parsley all work well.

# CHICKPEA "TUNA" SALAD

**GLUTEN-FREE, NUT-FREE, SOY-FREE, VEGETARIAN**

This is an easy vegetarian meal kids love. Packed with plant-based protein and a few simple vegetables, it's great on bread or crackers for lunch or as an entrée for dinner. It's also great to take on picnics.

**PREP TIME:**
15 MINUTES

**SERVES 4**

1 (15-ounce) can chickpeas, drained and rinsed

½ cup diced celery

½ red bell pepper, finely diced

½ cup mayonnaise

2 tablespoons minced onion

1 tablespoon sweet relish

1 tablespoon yellow mustard

2 teaspoons freshly squeezed lemon juice

1 teaspoon dried dill

¼ teaspoon sea salt

¼ teaspoon ground white pepper

¼ teaspoon smoked paprika

→ In a medium bowl, use a fork to mash the chickpeas gently. Add the celery, red bell pepper, mayonnaise, onion, relish, mustard, lemon juice, dill, salt, pepper, and paprika. Mix well and serve.

**MAKE IT YOUR OWN:** If your child is not allergic to tree nuts, add ½ cup slivered almonds, which give this dish some extra crunch.

# GREEN EGG FRITTATA WITH KALE, TOMATO, AND ONION

This recipe is inspired by a recipe my sister-in-law shared with me. She was trying to get her kids to eat more vegetables, and blending them with eggs was the jackpot. It's been a favorite for us ever since. Serve this with a side of Baked Potato Wedges with "Special Sauce" (page 63) for a complete meal.

**PREP TIME:**
15 MINUTES

**COOK TIME:**
40 MINUTES,
PLUS
10 MINUTES
TO REST

**SERVES 4**

Nonstick cooking spray

8 large eggs

2 cups kale or fresh spinach, stemmed

1 large Roma tomato, halved

¼ onion

⅓ cup dairy-free plain yogurt

2 tablespoons all-purpose flour

½ teaspoon sea salt

Freshly ground black pepper

⅓ cup shredded vegan cheddar cheese

Organic ketchup, for serving

1. Preheat the oven to 325°F. Lightly coat a 9-inch pie dish with cooking spray.

2. In a high-speed blender, combine the eggs, kale, tomato, onion, yogurt, flour, and salt. Season with pepper to taste and blend until well combined. Pour the egg mixture into the prepared pie dish.

3. Bake for about 40 minutes, or until the center is set.

4. Top with the cheese. Let sit for about 10 minutes before drizzling the top with ketchup to serve.

**SIMPLIFY IT:** Make family dinners a breeze by cooking this on the weekend, omitting the cheese, and simply reheating for breakfast, lunch, or dinner during the week. When you are ready to reheat, sprinkle the cheese over the top and bake at 325°F, covered, for 20 minutes, or until heated through. Serve with ketchup.

# EGGPLANT MEATBALLS

NUT-FREE, SOY-FREE, VEGETARIAN

Ever wonder how to get kids to eat eggplant? Transform it into "meatballs." The eggplant has a flavorful meaty consistency. Serve the meatballs with ketchup for dipping, tossed Into spaghetti, or turn them into meatball sandwiches topped with warm tomato sauce.

**PREP TIME:**
15 MINUTES

**COOK TIME:**
45 MINUTES

**MAKES
16 MEAT-
BALLS (4 PER
SERVING)**

Nonstick cooking spray

½ teaspoon avocado oil

1 eggplant, cut into 1-inch pieces

1 cup panko bread crumbs

1 large egg, beaten

2 tablespoons chopped fresh basil

2 tablespoons nutritional yeast

½ teaspoon garlic powder

½ teaspoon sea salt

⅛ teaspoon freshly ground black pepper

1 (24-ounce) jar tomato sauce

1. Preheat the oven to 375°F. Line a baking sheet with aluminum foil and spray it with cooking spray.
2. In a large skillet over medium-high heat, heat the oil. Add the eggplant and cook for 10 to 12 minutes, or until the eggplant has softened. Transfer the cooked eggplant to a food processor and puree until smooth. Pour the puree into a large bowl.
3. Add the panko, beaten egg, basil, nutritional yeast, garlic powder, salt, and pepper. Mix well until a dough forms. Using a tablespoon, scoop the mixture into your clean hands and roll it into a ball. Place the meatball onto the prepared baking sheet and repeat with the remaining mixture.
4. Bake the meatballs for about 20 minutes until brown and firm.
5. In a large skillet over medium heat, combine the tomato sauce and cooked meatballs. Cook for 5 to 10 minutes, or until the sauce is warm. Serve immediately.

# RAINBOW CORN CAKES WITH LIME DIPPING SAUCE

VEGETARIAN

These colorful patties are baked instead of pan-fried, so you don't have to stand over the stove. Sauté the vegetables first to soften them. Adding the flour and panko helps bind the vegetables into patties. The final touch is a zesty dipping sauce to complement the sweet corn flavors.

**PREP TIME:**
15 MINUTES

**COOK TIME:**
45 MINUTES

**MAKES
8 PATTIES
(2 PER
SERVING)**

### FOR THE LIME SAUCE
½ cup dairy-free sour cream

2 teaspoons freshly squeezed lime juice

2 teaspoons honey

### FOR THE CORN CAKES
2 teaspoons olive oil

1 red bell pepper, finely diced

¼ cup finely diced yellow onion

¼ cup grated carrot

½ cup frozen peas, thawed

1 (16-ounce) bag frozen corn, thawed

¾ cup cornmeal

½ cup panko bread crumbs

1 teaspoon white vinegar

1 tablespoon vegan butter, melted

1 large egg

2 tablespoons mayonnaise

1 tablespoon chopped fresh chives, or
1 teaspoon dried chives or dried thyme, plus more for garnish

1 teaspoon baking powder

1 teaspoon sea salt

½ teaspoon paprika

¼ teaspoon freshly ground black pepper

### TO MAKE THE LIME SAUCE
1. In a small bowl, whisk the sour cream, lime juice, honey, and vinegar to blend. Whisk in the melted butter. Refrigerate until ready to use.

## TO MAKE THE CORN CAKES

2. Preheat the oven to 400°F. Line a baking sheet with parchment paper.

3. In a large sauté pan or skillet over medium heat, heat the oil. Add the red bell pepper, onion, and carrot. Sauté for about 5 minutes, or until the onion is translucent. Stir in the peas and corn and cook for 5 more minutes. Turn off the heat and transfer the vegetables to a large bowl.

4. Add the cornmeal, panko, egg, mayonnaise, chives, baking powder, salt, paprika, and pepper. Stir until well combined. Using your clean hands, form 8 patties of equal size and place them on the prepared baking sheet.

5. Bake for 15 minutes, flip the corn cakes, and bake for 10 to 15 minutes more, or until set.

6. Turn on the broiler and broil the patties for 1 to 2 minutes, or until the tops are slightly browned and crispy. Garnish with chives and serve with the lime sauce.

**SERVING SUGGESTION:** Serve the corn cakes with Cilantro-Lime Shredded Cabbage Slaw (page 48) or Glazed Carrots (page 60).

# CHICKPEA NUGGETS

**VEGETARIAN**

This vegetarian version of chicken nuggets uses chickpea batter coated in panko for crispy perfection. If you have one of those picky eaters who returns time and again to chicken nuggets, try this recipe for some fun and variety.

**PREP TIME:**
15 MINUTES

**COOK TIME:**
25 MINUTES

**MAKES
36 NUGGETS
(9 PER
SERVING)**

Nonstick cooking spray

1½ cups panko bread crumbs, divided

1 (15-ounce) can chickpeas, drained and rinsed

¾ cup dairy-free milk

2 tablespoons chopped onion

1 large egg

1 tablespoon chopped fresh Italian parsley

1 teaspoon baking powder

½ teaspoon dried oregano

½ teaspoon garlic powder

½ teaspoon sea salt

¼ teaspoon freshly ground black pepper

1. Preheat the oven to 400°F. Line a baking pan with parchment paper and lightly coat it with cooking spray.
2. Put ½ cup of panko into a small bowl.
3. In a high-speed blender, combine the remaining 1 cup of panko, chickpeas, milk, onion, egg, parsley, baking powder, oregano, garlic powder, salt, and pepper. Blend until smooth. Using a tablespoon, scoop some of the mixture into your clean hands and form it into a 1-inch log shape. Flatten the nugget slightly, then dip each side into the panko in the small bowl. Place each nugget on the prepared baking sheet and repeat with the remaining mixture.
4. Bake for 15 minutes, flip the nuggets, and bake for 10 minutes more, or until warm and slightly crisp. Serve immediately.

**DID YOU KNOW?** Chickpeas are dense when used alone as a base filling. Using baking powder with panko and egg creates a fluffier nugget.

# BEAN AND CHEESE TAQUITOS

**EGG-FREE, GLUTEN-FREE, VEGAN**

This recipe is courtesy of my husband. Kristopher is the Taquito King, and this is our children's favorite meal. Serve these with a side of Fresh Guacamole (page 118) and salsa or turn them into enchiladas by adding them to a large baking dish, smothering with enchilada sauce, and baking instead of frying. For a larger crowd, double or triple the recipe.

**PREP TIME:**
10 MINUTES

**COOK TIME:**
35 MINUTES

**MAKES
16 TAQUITOS
(4 PER
SERVING)**

16 (6-inch) corn tortillas

2 cups vegetarian refried beans

2 cups shredded vegan cheese or Homemade Shredding Cheese (page 174)

¼ cup avocado oil

1. Working in batches, put a stack of 5 or 6 tortillas in the microwave and cover them with a slightly damp paper towel. Microwave in 30-second increments until just warm and a bit of steam rises from the tortillas. Repeat until all tortillas are warmed.
2. Place the tortillas on a work surface and evenly divide the beans and cheese among them. Roll the tortillas and set them on a plate, seam-side down, until ready to cook.
3. In a large skillet over medium heat, heat the oil for about 2 minutes until it starts to bubble. Add 4 rolled tortillas to the skillet and cook for about 3 minutes per side, or until they start to brown. Remove and repeat with the remaining tortillas and filling.
4. Let cool slightly before serving.

**DID YOU KNOW?** Warming the tortillas before filling them prevents them from cracking and breaking when rolling. If you prefer to warm them in the oven, preheat the oven to 350°F. Wrap 8 tortillas in aluminum foil (so for this recipe you will have two foil packages of 8 tortillas each) and heat for 10 to 15 minutes.

# EASY EGG-FRIED RICE BOWLS

This is one of those really easy meals that takes minimal time to cook and the cleanup is nearly as easy. These bowls have a mix of marvelous flavors that do not overpower. Perfect for kids that like to keep food simple.

**PREP TIME:**
15 MINUTES

**COOK TIME:**
15 MINUTES

**SERVES 4**

2 tablespoons avocado oil, divided

2 carrots, finely diced

6 large eggs, beaten

½ cup frozen peas, thawed

3 tablespoons soy sauce

2 tablespoons rice vinegar

½ teaspoon sesame oil

4 cups cooked white rice or brown rice

1. In a large skillet over medium heat, heat 1 tablespoon of avocado oil. Add the carrots and cook for 5 to 7 minutes, or until slightly tender. Transfer the carrots to a small bowl.
2. Pour the remaining 1 tablespoon of avocado oil into the skillet and add the eggs. Cook, stirring regularly, for 2 to 3 minutes until the eggs are scrambled and cooked through.
3. Add the cooked carrots, peas, soy sauce, vinegar, sesame oil, and cooked rice. Cook for 3 minutes, stirring. Serve immediately.

**RECIPE TIP:** If your kids enjoy tofu, add it to this dish. Chop a 14-ounce block of marinated tofu or tempeh into fine pieces and cook for 10 minutes so any liquid evaporates. Add it to the eggs with the other ingredients in step 3.

# GRAIN-FREE TOMATO AND CHEESE FLATBREAD PIZZA

**EGG-FREE, GLUTEN-FREE, VEGAN**

Pizza nights in our home are our favorite Friday night foodie adventures. This pizza is a quick and easy one when you need dinner in a hurry. Make it fun by setting up a pizza station so the kids can make their own personal pizzas.

**PREP TIME:**
10 MINUTES

**COOK TIME:**
20 MINUTES

**SERVES 4**

1 recipe Grain-Free Flatbread dough (page 172), uncooked

Cassava flour, for dusting

¾ cup tomato sauce

1 cup shredded vegan mozzarella cheese

Optional toppings: fresh basil, dried oregano, cooked ground sausage, sliced olives, sliced mushrooms, fresh tomato slices, red pepper flakes, nutritional yeast, roasted red peppers

1. Preheat the oven to 500°F. Line a baking sheet with parchment paper.
2. Divide the dough into 4 disks. On a floured work surface, place one of the disks. Using a rolling pin, roll the dough into a rough circle about ¼ inch thick and transfer it to the prepared baking sheet. Repeat with the remaining dough disks.
3. Bake for 10 minutes.
4. Top each disk with 3 tablespoons of tomato sauce and ¼ cup of cheese along with any toppings you like. Bake for 5 to 8 minutes more, or until the cheese is melted and bubbly.

**SUBSTITUTION TIP:** If you don't have time to make the flatbread dough, use 1 (16-ounce) bag of prepared pizza dough or a 12-inch dairy-free frozen cauliflower crust.

# MACARONI AND CHEESE WITH PEAS

VEGETARIAN

Six out of seven days a week, my oldest asks for macaroni and cheese for dinner. It's his favorite. If your dairy-free kid loves mac 'n' cheese, what do you do? You do this! Packed full of cheesy flavors and a smooth creamy texture, this wholesome sauce is made with a blend of cashews, sweet potatoes, mayonnaise, and nutritional yeast flakes. To make it fun, let the kids choose their favorite noodles.

**PREP TIME:**
20 MINUTES, PLUS 3 HOURS TO SOAK

**COOK TIME:**
20 MINUTES

**SERVES 8**

1 cup raw unsalted cashews

1 cup filtered water

1 pound dried macaroni

1 sweet potato, peeled and cooked

1 cup dairy-free milk

½ cup mayonnaise

¼ cup nutritional yeast

½ teaspoon salt

½ teaspoon onion powder

¼ teaspoon garlic powder

1 cup frozen peas, thawed

1. In a medium bowl, combine the cashews and filtered water. Let soak for 3 hours, or overnight. Drain the cashews and rinse.

2. Fill a large stockpot two-thirds full of water. Bring the water to a boil over high heat. Pour in the macaroni and cook for 5 to 7 minutes, or until tender. Drain and return the pasta to the pot.

3. Meanwhile, in a high-speed blender, combine the drained cashews, sweet potato, milk, mayonnaise, nutritional yeast, salt, onion powder, and garlic powder and blend until smooth.

4. Put the pot of pasta over low heat and add the cashew sauce and peas. Stir to combine. Cook for 3 to 5 minutes until the peas are warmed.

**MAKE IT YOUR OWN:** For added protein, cut up 8 tofu hot dogs and add them in step 4 with the peas. Or, if your family eats meat products, use turkey dogs, hot dogs, or even 2 cups cubed ham. Simply heat until the protein is warm. To make this nut free, skip steps 1 and 3 and use Alfredo Sauce (page 171).

# BUTTERY PENNE PASTA WITH CARAMELIZED BUTTERNUT SQUASH

NUT-FREE, VEGETARIAN

This recipe is the ideal comfort food for kids, with noodles tossed in a buttery vegan sauce with sautéed butternut squash cubes.

**PREP TIME:**
20 MINUTES

**COOK TIME:**
30 MINUTES

**SERVES 4**

12 ounces dried penne pasta

6 tablespoons (¾ stick) vegan butter, divided

1 (3-pound) butternut squash peeled, seeded, and cut into ½-inch chunks

1 cup low-sodium vegetable broth

1 tablespoon maple syrup

2 teaspoons apple cider vinegar

1 teaspoon dried thyme

½ teaspoon onion powder

¼ teaspoon ground nutmeg

Sea salt

Freshly ground black pepper

2 tablespoons nutritional yeast

1. Fill a large stockpot two-thirds full of water. Bring the water to a boil over high heat. Pour in the penne and cook for 9 to 11 minutes, or until tender. Drain.

2. In a large skillet over medium-high heat, melt 3 tablespoons of butter. Add the squash cubes in a single layer, making sure they do not overlap. Cook for 5 minutes, or until the squash begins to brown. Flip and cook for 5 minutes more, or until slightly tender and slightly browned.

3. Add the vegetable broth, maple syrup, vinegar, thyme, onion powder, and nutmeg. Season with salt and pepper to taste. Cover the skillet and cook for 4 minutes, or until heated through. Remove the lid and cook for 5 minutes more, or until the squash is soft.

**4.** Add the cooked pasta to the pan with the remaining 3 tablespoons of butter. Toss to coat and incorporate the butter.

**5.** Sprinkle the nutritional yeast over the pasta and serve warm.

**MAKE IT YOUR OWN:** Mix this up by trying new shapes and kinds of pasta. Bowties, mini shells, and macaroni all work well with this recipe. Try quinoa, black bean, lentil, or chickpea pasta. You can also add 1 (14.5-ounce) can green beans, drained and rinsed, and 1 (15-ounce) can cannellini beans, drained and rinsed, for extra protein and fiber.

# BLACK BEAN AND SWEET POTATO CHILI

**ALLERGEN-FREE, EGG-FREE, GLUTEN-FREE, NUT-FREE, SOY-FREE, VEGAN**

This is a hearty meal made from simple pantry items and fresh vegetables, and it is great for a large crowd or for make-ahead meals. It's a versatile recipe the whole family will enjoy.

**PREP TIME:**
20 MINUTES

**COOK TIME:**
45 MINUTES

**SERVES 6**

1 tablespoon olive oil

2 poblano peppers, seeded and finely chopped

1 large onion, chopped

1 red bell pepper, finely chopped

3 tablespoons tomato paste

5 large sweet potatoes, peeled and cut into ½-inch cubes

3 (14.5-ounce) cans fire-roasted diced tomatoes, with their juices

3 (15-ounce) cans black beans, drained and rinsed

1½ cups low-sodium vegetable broth

1 tablespoon smoked paprika

1 tablespoon dried oregano

1 tablespoon ground coriander

1 tablespoon ground cumin

¼ cup freshly squeezed lime juice

Sea salt

Freshly ground black pepper

**1.** In a large stockpot over medium heat, heat the oil. Add the poblano peppers, onion, and red bell pepper. Cook for 8 to 10 minutes, or until the onion is translucent.

**2.** Stir in the tomato paste, sweet potatoes, tomatoes with their juices, black beans, vegetable broth, paprika, oregano, coriander, cumin, and lime juice.

**3.** Turn the heat to high and bring the chili to a boil. When the chili is boiling, reduce the heat to medium-low and cover the pot. Simmer for 20 to 30 minutes, or until the sweet potatoes are tender.

4. Using a potato masher, gently mash the chili to blend the flavors and thicken. Season with salt and pepper to taste.

**LEFTOVERS:** This makes a lot of chili and leftovers have several uses. You can freeze them for another time in a sealed bag for up to 3 months. Other ideas include reserving 1 cup to use in Chili Mac 'n' Cheese Bites (page 64) that week, or using the chili to make burritos another night. Using a slotted spoon to make sure most of the liquid is drained, fill the tortillas with the chili. Top with vegan shredded cheese, and wrap into a burrito. Heat and eat.

*chapter seven*

# SEAFOOD

# POPCORN SHRIMP

Shrimp is usually a favorite in our home, so I keep a bag of peeled, deveined shrimp in the freezer to whip up a quick meal like this. Try avocado or coconut oil when frying, as these oils can withstand higher temperatures better.

**PREP TIME:**
10 MINUTES

**COOK TIME:**
25 MINUTES

**SERVES 4**

1 cup all-purpose flour

¼ teaspoon sea salt

¼ teaspoon freshly ground black pepper

3 large eggs

2 cups panko bread crumbs

1 tablespoon Old Bay seasoning

12 ounces raw frozen peeled and deveined shrimp, thawed

Avocado oil

Lemon wedges, for serving

Cocktail sauce, for serving (optional)

1. Line a large plate with parchment paper. Line another large plate with a double layer of paper towels.

2. Set up a breading station with three small bowls. In the first bowl, stir together the flour, salt, and pepper. In the second bowl, whisk the eggs until they are well combined and a little frothy. In the third bowl, combine the panko and Old Bay seasoning.

3. Dip and thoroughly coat about 6 shrimp at a time in the flour, then the egg, and finally the seasoned panko. Set the breaded shrimp on the parchment-lined plate. Repeat until all the shrimp are breaded.

4. In a deep stockpot over medium-high heat, pour in the avocado oil until it reaches a 2-inch depth and heat the oil for about 5 minutes, or until it reaches 365°F.

**5.** Add about 5 shrimp and cook for 2 minutes. Flip the shrimp and cook for 2 minutes more, or until the shrimp are cooked through and golden brown. Transfer the crispy cooked shrimp to the paper-towel-lined plate to drain. Repeat with the remaining shrimp.

**6.** Serve immediately with a lemon wedge for squeezing and cocktail sauce for dipping (if using).

**SERVING SUGGESTION:** Serve these with Easy Egg-Fried Rice Bowls (page 78), Buttery Penne Pasta with Caramelized Butternut Squash (page 82), or Rainbow Corn Cakes with Lime Dipping Sauce (page 74).

# HALIBUT TACOS WITH CREAMY DRESSING

Being dairy free shouldn't mean skipping creamy dipping sauces! This sauce is silky and flavorful and complements the light, flaky halibut in these fun, tasty tacos. Feel free to try the recipe with flounder or cod, but reduce the cooking time in that case to 6 minutes, or until the fish flakes easily with a fork.

**PREP TIME:**
15 MINUTES

**COOK TIME:**
10 MINUTES

**SERVES 4**

### FOR THE DIPPING SAUCE

½ cup vegan mayonnaise

2 teaspoons honey

1 teaspoon freshly squeezed lime juice

1 teaspoon white vinegar

½ teaspoon ground coriander

½ teaspoon paprika

¼ teaspoon garlic salt

¼ teaspoon dried oregano

### FOR THE FISH

Nonstick cooking spray

4 (6-ounce) halibut fillets

1 teaspoon paprika

½ teaspoon sea salt

¼ teaspoon freshly ground black pepper

8 (6-inch) corn tortillas (soft or crispy)

1 lime, halved crosswise

1 cup shredded green cabbage

¼ cup chopped red bell pepper

2 tablespoons chopped fresh cilantro

### TO MAKE THE DIPPING SAUCE

**1.** In a small bowl, stir together the mayonnaise, honey, lime juice, vinegar, coriander, paprika, garlic salt, and oregano until well combined. Cover and refrigerate for up to 1 hour before serving.

## TO MAKE THE FISH

**2.** Position an oven rack 6 to 8 inches from the top of the oven and preheat the broiler. Coat the bottom of a 9-by-9-inch baking dish with cooking spray.

**3.** Place the fish in the prepared baking dish and season it on both sides with paprika, salt, and pepper.

**4.** Broil the fish for 6 to 8 minutes, turning once, or until the fish flakes easily with a fork.

**5.** Meanwhile, warm the tortillas in the microwave in two batches. Heat a stack of 4 tortillas, covered by a slightly damp paper towel, on high power in 30-second increments until just warm and a bit of steam rises from the tortillas. Repeat.

**6.** When the fish is cooked, squeeze half the lime over the fish. Cut the fish into slices, or break it into bite-size pieces.

**7.** Layer each warmed tortilla with cabbage followed by fish. Drizzle the sauce over the fish and garnish with red bell pepper, cilantro, and the juice from the remaining lime half.

**MAKE IT YOUR OWN:** Convert this recipe into a refreshing grain bowl. Add cooked rice or quinoa to a bowl and top with sliced red bell pepper, cabbage, and cilantro. Break apart the halibut and add it to the bowl. Season with salt and pepper to taste and drizzle the dipping sauce on top.

# SHRIMP AND AVOCADO CEVICHE

Serve this fun, colorful dish with "scoop" tortilla chips and have the kids spoon or scoop it into them. The ceviche is ready in as little as 30 minutes and is a bright, citrusy meal the whole family will enjoy.

**PREP TIME:**
10 MINUTES

**COOK TIME:**
10 MINUTES, PLUS 1 HOUR TO CHILL

**SERVES 4**

1 tablespoon olive oil

1 garlic clove, minced

¼ cup freshly squeezed lime juice

2 tablespoons freshly squeezed lemon juice

1 tablespoon freshly squeezed orange juice

¼ teaspoon sea salt

¼ teaspoon freshly ground black pepper

1 pound frozen peeled and deveined baby shrimp, thawed

½ teaspoon onion powder

4 Roma tomatoes, diced

¾ cup frozen shelled edamame, thawed and steamed according to the package directions

½ cup fresh or frozen sweet corn kernels, thawed

1 avocado, peeled, halved, pitted, and diced

⅓ cup fresh cilantro, chopped

Scoop tortilla chips, for serving

1. In a medium saucepan over low heat, heat the oil. Add the garlic and cook for about 3 minutes until fragrant. Add the lime juice, lemon juice, orange juice, salt, pepper, and shrimp. Cook for 2 to 4 minutes, or until the shrimp have turned pink. Remove from the heat and transfer the shrimp and pan juices to a large bowl. Let cool slightly.
2. Stir in the onion powder, tomatoes, edamame, corn, avocado, and cilantro. Refrigerate for 45 minutes to 1 hour to chill. Serve cold with chips for scooping.

**SERVING SUGGESTION:** For a complete meal, serve the ceviche with Zucchini Fries (page 58).

# CRISPY BREADED FISH STICKS

This is a great recipe to use up the crumbs and broken pieces at the bottom of a tortilla chip bag. Add the chips to a food processor and gently blend into crumbs. They make a tasty substitute for bread crumbs and a crispy coating for baked cod fillets.

**PREP TIME:**
10 MINUTES

**COOK TIME:**
20 MINUTES

**SERVES 4**

Nonstick cooking spray

1 pound cod fillets, cut into 1-inch strips

Sea salt

Freshly ground black pepper

1½ cups tortilla chips

½ teaspoon smoked paprika

1 cup all-purpose flour

2 large eggs

1. Preheat the oven to 400°F. Line a baking sheet with aluminum foil and spray it with cooking spray.
2. Lightly season the fish all over with salt and pepper.
3. In a food processor, lightly blend the tortilla chips and paprika to form a thick crumb, but don't overprocess.
4. Set up a breading station with three small bowls. Put the flour into the first bowl. In the second bowl, whisk the eggs until they are well combined and a little frothy. Transfer the tortilla chips to the third bowl.
5. Dip and thoroughly coat each fish stick in the flour, then the eggs, and finally the tortilla chips. Set the breaded fish sticks on the prepared baking sheet in a single layer and lightly coat with cooking spray.
6. Bake for 8 minutes. Turn the fish sticks over and coat with cooking spray. Bake for 8 minutes more, or until the fish flakes easily with a fork. Transfer the cooked fish to a serving tray and serve immediately.

# COD BAKED IN PARCHMENT

**EGG-FREE, GLUTEN-FREE, NUT-FREE, SOY-FREE**

Baking fish in a foil envelope makes doing dishes a breeze! Lemon gives this fish a nice tang and the cooked tomatoes add a touch of sweetness. Serve with Simple Roasted Vegetables (page 66) for a fuss-free meal.

**PREP TIME:**
10 MINUTES

**COOK TIME:**
15 MINUTES

**SERVES 4**

1 lemon, cut into slices

½ white onion, cut into slices

1½ pounds fresh cod

¼ teaspoon garlic powder

½ teaspoon sea salt

Freshly ground black pepper

2 tablespoons finely chopped fresh parsley

½ cup grape tomatoes

1. Preheat the oven to 400°F. Tear off a sheet of parchment paper or aluminum foil large enough to envelop the fish and vegetables. Lay the sheet loosely atop a baking sheet.
2. Spread the lemon slices and onion on the parchment, then lay the cod on top. Sprinkle with the garlic powder, salt, a bit of pepper, and the fresh parsley. Sprinkle the tomatoes over the fish. Fold in the parchment over the fish and vegetables and fold closed on top and the sides. (The envelope will remain on the baking sheet.)
3. Bake for 10 to 12 minutes, or until the fish is cooked and flakes easily with a fork.
4. Open the parchment slowly and carefully to avoid the hot steam. Serve immediately.

**SERVING SUGGESTION:** For another complete meal option, serve the cod with rice pilaf, Crispy Sautéed Green Beans (page 57), or Glazed Carrots (page 60).

# BAKED SALMON NUGGETS

NUT-FREE, SOY-FREE

Crispy outside and soft inside, this tasty cross between fish sticks and chicken nuggets is a great way to mix up your weeknight dinner repertoire. Serve with cocktail sauce or creamy dill sauce (see Salmon with Creamy Dill Sauce, page 97) and a side of Creamy Mashed Cauliflower (page 62) or Simple Roasted Vegetables (page 66) to round out the meal.

**PREP TIME:**
20 MINUTES

**COOK TIME:**
25 MINUTES

**MAKES ABOUT 32 NUGGETS (8 PER SERVING)**

2 (5-ounce) cans boneless, skinless pink salmon in water, drained

¼ cup finely diced onion

¼ cup finely diced red bell pepper

½ cup panko bread crumbs

1 teaspoon Old Bay seasoning

½ teaspoon dried parsley

½ teaspoon baking powder

1 tablespoon chopped fresh chives, or 1 teaspoon dried chives

1 tablespoon mayonnaise

1 large egg

2 teaspoons freshly squeezed lemon juice

Sea salt

Freshly ground black pepper

1. Preheat the oven to 400°F. Fit a wire cooling rack over a baking sheet.

2. In a large bowl, combine the salmon, onion, red bell pepper, panko, Old Bay seasoning, parsley, baking powder, chives, mayonnaise, egg, and lemon juice. Season with salt and pepper to taste. Using a fork, break up the salmon and mix the ingredients well until they pull together into a sticky doughlike consistency. Using a tablespoon, scoop some of the mixture into your clean hands and form it into a nugget shape. Place the nugget on the wire rack. Repeat with the remaining mixture.

3. Bake the nuggets for 15 minutes, flip, and bake for 10 minutes more, or until lightly golden. Serve immediately.

# PAN-SEARED MAPLE-GLAZED SALMON

Salmon is one of the best seafoods to consume, as it is loaded with omega-3 fatty oils that promote a healthy brain and heart. This is especially important in young children, as their brains are actively taking in and learning new information daily.

**PREP TIME:**
10 MINUTES,
PLUS 30
MINUTES
TO MARINATE

**COOK TIME:**
10 MINUTES

**SERVES 4**

2 tablespoons maple syrup

1 tablespoon extra-virgin olive oil

2 teaspoons apple cider vinegar

1 teaspoon paprika

½ teaspoon ground cumin

½ teaspoon garlic salt

½ teaspoon freshly ground black pepper

4 (6-ounce) skin-on salmon fillets

2 tablespoons vegan butter

1. In a medium bowl, stir together the maple syrup, oil, vinegar, paprika, cumin, garlic salt, and pepper. Reserve 1½ tablespoons.
2. Put the salmon in a 9-by-13-inch baking dish and pour the marinade (minus the reserved 1½ tablespoons) on top. Cover and refrigerate to marinate for at least 30 minutes and up to 1 hour.
3. Preheat the oven to 425°F.
4. In a large ovenproof skillet over medium-high heat, melt the butter, swirling it to coat the skillet.
5. Remove the salmon from the marinade, discarding the marinade. Place the salmon in the skillet, skin-side up. Cook for 2 minutes. Turn the salmon and brush each fillet with the reserved marinade.
6. Place the skillet in the oven and roast the salmon for 8 minutes, or until the top is browned and the flesh is opaque and flakes easily with a fork.

**DID YOU KNOW?** Buy good fish from a sustainable source. Good-quality seafood should be odorless.

# SALMON WITH CREAMY DILL SAUCE

This is a simple salmon recipe without any fluff, just a delicate creamy dill sauce. Serve with a fresh green salad, Simple Roasted Vegetables (page 66), Glazed Carrots (page 60), Broccoli Tots (page 61), or Crispy Sautéed Green Beans (page 57).

**PREP TIME:**
10 MINUTES

**COOK TIME:**
10 MINUTES

**SERVES 4**

½ cup mayonnaise

½ cup vegan sour cream or plain yogurt

½ cup chopped fresh dill

1 tablespoon freshly squeezed lemon juice

½ teaspoon onion powder

Sea salt

Freshly ground black pepper

2 tablespoons vegan butter

4 (6-ounce) skin-on salmon fillets

1. Preheat the oven to 425°F.
2. In a small bowl, whisk the mayonnaise, sour cream, dill, lemon juice, and onion powder to blend. Season with salt and pepper to taste and whisk again. Cover and refrigerate until ready to use.
3. In a large ovenproof skillet over medium-high heat, melt the butter, swirling it to coat the skillet. Place the salmon in the skillet, skin-side up, and season with salt and pepper to taste. Cook for 2 minutes. Turn the salmon.
4. Place the skillet in the oven and roast for 8 minutes, or until the top is browned and the flesh is opaque and flakes easily with a fork. Serve topped with the creamy dill sauce.

**DID YOU KNOW?** Cook the salmon until opaque yet still moist and flaky. It can become dry when overcooked.

# SWORDFISH KABOBS

When summer comes, these skewers are great to make outdoors with seasonal peppers and squash. It is a colorful dish that you can get the kids involved in creating by having them make their own skewers. Serve it with cocktail sauce or with Lime Dipping Sauce (page 74).

**PREP TIME:**
10 MINUTES,
PLUS 30
MINUTES
TO MARINATE

**COOK TIME:**
10 MINUTES

**MAKES
6 SKEWERS**

1 pound wild-caught swordfish steak, skin removed, cut into 2-inch cubes

¼ teaspoon ground coriander

¼ teaspoon sea salt

Freshly ground black pepper

¼ cup olive oil, plus more for the grill

1 green bell pepper

1 yellow bell pepper

1 red or orange bell pepper

1 yellow squash

1 zucchini

½ small red onion

½ cup grape tomatoes

Lemon or lime wedges, for serving

1. If you are using wooden skewers, soak them in water for 30 minutes.

2. In a large zip-top bag, combine the cubed fish, coriander, salt, a grind of pepper, and the oil. Tightly seal the bag, then gently tip the bag back and forth so the marinade coats the fish. Refrigerate for 30 minutes.

3. Meanwhile, prepare the vegetables: Cut off the tops and remove the seeds from the green, yellow, and red bell peppers. Cut the peppers into 2-inch squares. Cut the yellow squash and zucchini into 1-inch slices. Cut the red onion into 2-inch square chunks.

4. Rub the grill with a bit of oil to prevent the food from sticking. Preheat the grill to medium heat.

**5.** Make the skewers by alternating two or three vegetables, including the tomatoes, then a piece of fish, then two or three more vegetables, then a piece of fish, and so on. (There should be two or three pieces of fish per skewer.) Use any remaining vegetables to make a vegetable skewer. Drizzle the leftover oil from the bag over the skewers and use your hands to coat the vegetables and fish with the oil.

**6.** Grill the skewers for 4 minutes, flip, and grill for 3 to 5 minutes more until the fish is opaque and slightly flaky with grill marks. Serve with lemon or lime wedges for squeezing.

**DID YOU KNOW?** Soaking wooden skewers in water for at least 30 minutes helps prevent them from catching fire while grilling.

# ITALIAN TUNA CASSEROLE

This incredibly easy tuna casserole can be made with pantry items. It has an Italian twist, as it is tossed with a marinara sauce instead of cream sauce. When I was a kid, my mom would make this all the time, and I remember loving the sweet tomato sauce with salty tuna blended in. You can either leave the tuna in thick chunks or break it up into small pieces that blend in with the noodles and sauce, depending on what your family prefers.

**PREP TIME:**
10 MINUTES

**COOK TIME:**
25 MINUTES

**SERVES 6**

Nonstick cooking spray

1 (12-ounce) package penne pasta

2 (5-ounce) cans albacore tuna in water, drained

1 (24-ounce) jar marinara sauce

1 teaspoon onion powder

½ teaspoon garlic powder

½ teaspoon dried basil

¼ teaspoon dried oregano

1½ cups shredded vegan mozzarella cheese, divided

1 tablespoon chopped fresh parsley

1. Preheat the oven to 400°F. Lightly coat a 9-by-13-inch baking dish with cooking spray.
2. Fill a large stockpot two-thirds full of water. Bring the water to a boil over high heat. Pour in the penne and cook for 9 to 11 minutes, or until tender. Drain.
3. In a large bowl, combine the tuna, marinara sauce, onion powder, garlic powder, basil, oregano, and 1 cup of mozzarella cheese. Mix well. Add the cooked pasta and stir until well coated. Pour the mixture into the prepared baking dish.
4. Top with the remaining ½ cup of cheese.

**5.** Cover the dish with aluminum foil and bake for 10 minutes, or until warmed through and the cheese is melted. Remove from the oven and garnish with parsley. Serve immediately.

**SIMPLIFY IT:** To save time, make this in advance earlier in the week but do not bake it. Cover the casserole dish and place it in the refrigerator for up to 4 days. When you are ready to eat, heat the casserole in the oven at 350°F for 20 minutes, or until it is heated through and the cheese is melty.

*chapter eight*

# POULTRY

# CLASSIC CHICKEN NUGGETS

**NUT-FREE, SOY-FREE**

An all-time favorite food for kids. There is one thing that never fails with my boys and that is serving them chicken nuggets—they eat every last bite. Even my youngest, who is going through an anti-chicken phase, will eat these. Baking instead of frying keeps them healthy and easy.

**PREP TIME:**
10 MINUTES

**COOK TIME:**
25 MINUTES

**MAKES
20 NUGGETS
(5 PER
SERVING)**

2 large eggs

1 cup panko bread crumbs

½ teaspoon garlic powder

½ teaspoon smoked paprika

¼ teaspoon salt

¼ teaspoon freshly ground black pepper

8 ounces boneless, skinless chicken breast, cut into (about 20) 1-inch pieces

Nonstick cooking spray

1. Preheat the oven to 425°F. Fit a wire cooling rack over a baking sheet.

2. Set up a breading station with two small bowls. In the first bowl, whisk the eggs until they are well combined and a little frothy. In the second bowl, stir together the panko, garlic powder, paprika, salt, and pepper.

3. Dip and thoroughly coat each piece of chicken in the egg, then in the breading. Set the breaded chicken on the wire rack in a single layer.

4. Coat the nuggets with cooking spray.

5. Bake for 15 minutes. Flip the nuggets and coat them with cooking spray. Bake for 8 to 10 minutes more, or until the breading is browned. Let cool slightly before serving.

**SIMPLIFY IT:** This recipe freezes well, so you may want to double or triple it. Place the cooked nuggets in a sealed freezer bag and keep frozen for up to 1 month. Pull the nuggets out of the freezer just before dinner and bake them at 425°F for 10 to 12 minutes, flipping once halfway through the cooking time.

# HONEY MUSTARD CHICKEN WINGS

**GLUTEN-FREE, NUT-FREE, SOY-FREE**

There is something about the combination of sweet and salty that kids love. These chicken wings are tossed in honey mustard sauce and baked to crispy perfection. Serve these wings along with Tangy Corn, Tomato, and Chickpea Salad (page 50) or Baked Potato Wedges with "Special Sauce" (page 63).

**PREP TIME:**
15 MINUTES

**COOK TIME:**
45 MINUTES

**MAKES 8 TO 10 WINGS (2 PER SERVING)**

1½ pounds party-size chicken wings

½ teaspoon smoked paprika

½ teaspoon garlic powder

¼ teaspoon sea salt

1½ tablespoons avocado oil

2 batches Honey Mustard Sauce (page 168), or 1 cup store-bought honey mustard sauce, divided

1. Preheat the oven to 400°F. Line a large sheet pan with parchment paper.
2. Dry off the wings by patting them down with paper towels.
3. In a small bowl, stir together the paprika, garlic powder, and salt.
4. Using a pastry brush or basting brush, lightly coat the wings with oil. Sprinkle the seasoning mix over the wings on both sides. Place the wings, evenly spaced, on the prepared baking sheet.
5. Bake for 25 minutes.
6. Use the same pastry brush or a basting brush to coat the wings with half the honey mustard sauce. Bake for 20 more minutes until the wings are browned on top and reach an internal temperature of 165°F. (For extra-crispy wings, turn on the broiler and broil for 3 to 5 minutes, or until the desired crispiness is achieved.)
7. Serve with the remaining honey mustard sauce for dipping.

# BARBECUE CHICKEN BAGEL PIZZAS

As a kid growing up in the 1980s my siblings and I loved frozen bagel snacks. They were our go-to after-school recipe or an easy weeknight dinner. Always check the label when purchasing prepared ingredients.

**PREP TIME:**
10 MINUTES

**COOK TIME:**
10 MINUTES

**SERVES 4
(2 BAGEL
PIZZAS
EACH)**

4 bagels, halved

½ cup barbecue sauce

¾ cup shredded vegan mozzarella cheese

⅓ cup diced cooked chicken

Chopped fresh cilantro, for garnish

1. Preheat the oven to 425°F. Line a baking sheet with parchment paper.
2. Place each bagel half, cut-side up, on the prepared baking sheet. Spread about 2 tablespoons of barbecue sauce over each. Sprinkle with cheese, then top with chicken.
3. Bake for 10 minutes, or until the cheese melts.
4. Garnish with cilantro and serve.

**MAKE IT YOUR OWN:** Skip the suggested toppings here and use your children's favorite toppings, whether tomato sauce, pepperoni slices, fresh basil, mushrooms, or olives. The possibilities are endless!

# SKILLET CHICKEN QUESADILLAS

My kids constantly request quesadillas. My husband is the expert quesadilla maker in our household, and these are the quesadillas he makes to keep the kids happy whenever the request comes in.

**PREP TIME:**
5 MINUTES

**COOK TIME:**
25 MINUTES

**SERVES 4**

Nonstick cooking spray

8 (8-inch) flour tortillas, or 16 (6-inch) corn tortillas

1 cup shredded vegan cheddar cheese or Homemade Shredding Cheese (page 174)

1 cup finely diced cooked chicken

2 teaspoons mild taco seasoning

1. Preheat the oven to 170°F. Lightly coat a baking sheet with cooking spray and place it in the oven.
2. Lightly coat a large skillet with cooking spray and heat it over medium-high heat.
3. Place 1 flour tortilla, or 2 corn tortillas, in the skillet. Sprinkle with ¼ cup of cheese, ¼ cup of chicken, and a sprinkle of taco seasoning. Top with a second tortilla.
4. Cook for 2 minutes, turn, and cook for 2 to 3 minutes more until slightly golden on each side and the cheese has melted. Place the cooked quesadilla on the baking sheet in the oven to keep warm. Repeat with the remaining tortillas and filling.
5. Cut each quesadilla into 4 wedges to serve.

**MAKE IT YOUR OWN:** Customize the quesadilla with what your children like. Swap the chicken for beans or add small pieces of cooked broccoli florets. Top with fresh avocado slices, salsa, or Fresh Guacamole (page 118).

# SWEET-AND-SOUR CHICKEN

**EGG-FREE, GLUTEN-FREE**

This wholesome recipe is made without breading and coated with a sweet-and-sour sticky sauce. My son's favorite school hot lunch is sweet-and-sour orange chicken and this version is much healthier, more flavorful, and a breeze to make—without processed ingredients. Serve it over rice.

**PREP TIME:**
15 MINUTES

**COOK TIME:**
20 MINUTES

**SERVES 4**

**FOR THE SAUCE**
¾ cup coconut sugar
or light brown sugar

½ cup apple cider vinegar

⅓ cup organic ketchup

¼ cup tamari or
gluten-free soy sauce

1½ tablespoons sesame oil

3 garlic cloves, minced

1 tablespoon cornstarch

1 tablespoon water

**FOR THE CHICKEN**
¼ cup cornstarch

½ teaspoon paprika

½ teaspoon
baking powder

Sea salt

Freshly ground
black pepper

1¼ pounds boneless,
skinless chicken breast
cut into 1-inch pieces

2 tablespoons olive oil

1 scallion, green
part only, diced

Sesame seeds, for garnish

**TO MAKE THE SAUCE**

**1.** In a medium saucepan over high heat, whisk the coconut sugar, vinegar, ketchup, tamari, sesame oil, and garlic. Bring to a boil, then reduce the heat to low.

**2.** In a small bowl, whisk the cornstarch and water until dissolved, then whisk the slurry into the sauce. Keep the sauce at a low simmer while you make the chicken.

## TO MAKE THE CHICKEN

**3.** In a large zip-top bag, combine the cornstarch, paprika, baking powder, and a pinch each of salt and pepper. Make sure the mixture is well combined, then add the chicken pieces. Seal the bag and toss the chicken in the bag until all pieces are coated.

**4.** In a large skillet over medium-high heat, heat the oil. Add the chicken and cook for 4 minutes, flip, and cook for 3 minutes more, or until cooked through and no longer pink.

**5.** Pour the sauce into the pan and stir to coat the chicken. Cover the skillet and cook for 3 to 5 minutes to thicken the sauce and ensure the meat is fully cooked.

**6.** Garnish with scallion and sesame seeds.

**DID YOU KNOW?** Coconut sugar is not as processed as granulated sugar and it has a lower glycemic index. That doesn't mean you can go wild with it, but it does have some benefits over granulated sugar. If you don't have access to coconut sugar, do a 1:1 replacement with organic cane sugar, brown sugar, or granulated sugar.

# TORTILLA-CRUSTED CHICKEN TENDERS

**NUT-FREE, SOY-FREE**

With this dish, you'll have happy kids. How could they not be, when the two main ingredients are chicken and chips? Tortilla chips are pulsed with seasonings and used as a crispy breading for baked chicken strips. They are ready in about 35 minutes. Serve with Honey Mustard Sauce (page 168), ketchup, or Baked Potato Wedges with "Special Sauce" (page 63).

**PREP TIME:**
15 MINUTES

**COOK TIME:**
20 MINUTES

**SERVES 4**

Nonstick cooking spray

1½ pounds (8 to 10) chicken tenders

Sea salt

Freshly ground black pepper

1½ cups tortilla chips, crumbled

2 teaspoons Italian seasoning

½ teaspoon garlic powder

1 cup all-purpose flour

2 large eggs

1. Preheat the oven to 400°F. Line a baking sheet with aluminum foil and coat it with cooking spray.
2. Season the chicken tenders all over with salt and pepper.
3. In a food processor, combine the tortilla chips, Italian seasoning, and garlic powder. Lightly blend to form a thick crumb, but don't overprocess.
4. Set up a breading station with three small bowls. Put the flour into the first bowl. In the second bowl, whisk the eggs until they are well combined and a little frothy. Transfer the tortilla chips to the third bowl.
5. Dip and thoroughly coat each chicken tender in the flour, then the egg, and finally the tortillas. Set the breaded chicken on the prepared baking sheet in a single layer. Coat the tenders with cooking spray.

6. Bake for 8 minutes. Flip the tenders and coat with cooking spray. Bake for 8 to 10 minutes more, or until the chicken is cooked through. Serve immediately.

**SERVING SUGGESTION:** These chicken tenders are endlessly versatile. Serve them with warm marinara sauce for dipping, or chopped up over pasta for a complete meal.

# CREAM OF CHICKEN AND BROCCOLI CASSEROLE

**SOY-FREE**

My kids love creamy dishes and this recipe combines all the flavors of canned "cream of chicken" tossed in pasta in a great dairy-free meal. Start by opening a can of coconut cream and mixing the solids and liquids together, then chill it before adding to the roux. It will stay mixed after it is opened, but for best results, you want it chilled. At the same time, put the chicken broth in the refrigerator to chill.

**PREP TIME:**
15 MINUTES

**COOK TIME:**
45 MINUTES

**6 SERVINGS**

10 ounces dried penne pasta

2 cups broccoli florets

4 cups diced cooked chicken

Sea salt

Freshly ground black pepper

3 tablespoons avocado oil or vegan butter

1 tablespoon freshly squeezed lemon juice

2 garlic cloves, minced

3 tablespoons all-purpose flour

⅔ cup coconut milk, mixed and chilled (see headnote)

⅔ cup low-sodium chicken broth, chilled

1 tablespoon nutritional yeast

½ teaspoon ground nutmeg

1. Fill a large stockpot two-thirds full of water. Bring the water to a boil over high heat. Pour in the penne and cook for 9 to 11 minutes, or until tender. Drain, then transfer to a 9-by-13-inch baking dish.
2. Preheat the oven to 375°F.
3. Add the broccoli and chicken to the pasta and season with salt and pepper. Mix well.
4. In a medium skillet over medium heat, combine the oil, lemon juice, and garlic. Cook for 1 to 2 minutes until the garlic becomes fragrant.

**5.** Add the flour and a pinch each of salt and pepper. Mix until smooth. Cook for 2 minutes, stirring frequently, until the mixture is a bubbly thick paste. Continue to cook for about 5 minutes more, stirring, being careful to make sure the roux does not burn, until the roux is a light golden color.

**6.** Slowly stir in the chilled coconut milk and chicken broth. Add the nutritional yeast and nutmeg and stir while the sauce thickens. Pour the sauce over the noodle mixture and stir until well combined.

**7.** Cover the dish with aluminum foil and bake for 20 minutes until set and warmed through.

**SUBSTITUTION TIP:** To make this recipe gluten free substitute gluten-free pasta for the penne and use gluten-free flour instead of wheat flour.

# CHICKEN À LA KING

**EGG-FREE**

A beautiful, creamy chicken dish with vegetables. Serve over noodles or rice, or with a baked potato.

**PREP TIME:**
15 MINUTES

**COOK TIME:**
15 MINUTES

**SERVES 6**

5 tablespoons plus 1 teaspoon vegan butter

1 small sweet onion, diced

½ cup diced carrot

¼ cup diced celery

½ cup diced mushrooms

¾ teaspoon sea salt

½ teaspoon freshly ground black pepper

¼ teaspoon poultry seasoning

⅓ cup all-purpose flour

2 cups coconut milk

½ cup low-sodium chicken broth

1 cup frozen peas, thawed

3 cups shredded rotisserie chicken

½ cup pimientos

1. In a large skillet over medium-high heat, melt the butter. Add the onion, carrot, celery, and mushrooms. Cook for 5 to 7 minutes until the onion is translucent and the mushrooms are soft. Add the salt, pepper, and poultry seasoning. Sprinkle the flour over the vegetable mixture. Cook for 2 minutes, stirring.

2. Slowly add the coconut milk and chicken broth, whisking to combine.

3. Add the peas and chicken. Simmer for about 1 minute until thickened. Stir in the pimientos and serve.

**MAKE IT YOUR OWN:** This dish resembles a thick yet creamy potpie filling and can be used as just that. Fill a prebaked 9-inch dairy-free pastry crust with the mixture and bake at 350°F for about 10 minutes, or until the crust and filling are heated through.

# HONEY MUSTARD TURKEY SLIDERS

These sliders are fabulous to serve the family for a Sunday brunch or lunch after church with your favorite sides. Using store-bought rolls makes this easy and toasting them in the oven makes them softer. These sliders are flavored with my honey mustard sauce that kids adore. This is also a wonderful way to use leftover holiday turkey—thinly slice the leftovers and use instead of deli turkey.

**PREP TIME:**
10 MINUTES

**COOK TIME:**
20 MINUTES

**SERVES 4**

Nonstick cooking spray

8 dairy-free mini dinner rolls

1 batch Honey Mustard Sauce (page 168)

8 thin slices vegan cheese or 1 cup Homemade Shredding Cheese (page 174)

8 slices thinly sliced deli turkey

1. Preheat the oven to 350°F. Lightly coat a 9-by-9-inch baking dish with cooking spray.
2. Arrange the bottom halves of the rolls, cut-side up, in the baking dish. Smear the bottoms of the rolls with honey mustard sauce. Layer on the cheese and turkey. Top with the top halves of the rolls.
3. Cover the baking dish with aluminum foil and bake for 20 minutes to warm. Serve immediately with any extra sauce for dipping.

**SERVING SUGGESTION:** Serve with Broccoli Tots (page 61) or Tangy Corn, Tomato, and Chickpea Salad (page 50).

# MINI TURKEY MEATBALLS WITH STEAMED BROCCOLI

This recipe is all about speedy scratch cooking. Mixing everything in one bowl, then leaving it to bake makes mealtime a breeze. I like to add a bit of tomato sauce to the meatballs to give them a naturally sweet kick kids enjoy. Serve the meatballs with steamed broccoli for a balanced, wholesome meal.

**PREP TIME:**
15 MINUTES

**COOK TIME:**
35 MINUTES

**MAKES 24 MEAT BALLS (6 PER SERVING)**

2 tablespoons avocado oil

1½ pounds ground turkey

½ cup tomato sauce, plus more for serving (optional)

¾ cup old-fashioned rolled oats

1 large egg, beaten

¼ yellow onion, minced

¼ cup grated carrot

1 teaspoon sea salt, plus more for seasoning

½ teaspoon freshly ground black pepper, plus more for seasoning

2 cups broccoli florets

1. Preheat the oven to 350°F. Line a baking sheet with parchment paper.
2. Put the oil in a small bowl.
3. In a large bowl, combine the ground turkey, tomato sauce, oats, egg, onion, carrot, salt, and pepper. Using your clean hands or a wooden spoon, mix until well blended and a bit sticky. Scoop a small spoonful of meat into your hands and roll it into a 1-inch-diameter meatball. Dip the meatball into the oil and rub the oil around the meatball with your hands. Place the meatball on the prepared baking sheet. Repeat with the remaining mixture. Space the meatballs about 1½ inches apart on the baking sheet.
4. Bake for 30 minutes, rolling the meatballs over every 10 minutes to brown on all sides.

**5.** About 5 minutes before the meatballs are finished, put 1 inch of water and a steamer basket into a large pot and bring the water to a boil. Add the broccoli, cover the pot, and cook for 3 to 5 minutes until slightly tender. Remove from the steamer and season with salt and pepper.

**6.** Serve the broccoli with the meatballs and extra tomato sauce for dipping, if desired.

**LEFTOVERS:** Add leftover meatballs to pasta dishes, chop them for topping pizza, slice the meatballs into soup, or use the meatballs instead of sausage in the Sausage and Potato Breakfast Burritos (page 38).

# TURKEY TACO BOWLS WITH FRESH GUACAMOLE

EGG-FREE, GLUTEN-FREE

These taco bowls are a true crowd-pleaser. They can be individualized so everyone in the family can have a choice of their favorite toppings, including fresh homemade guacamole.

**PREP TIME:**
15 MINUTES

**COOK TIME:**
25 MINUTES,
PLUS
10 MINUTES
TO REST

**SERVES 6**

## FOR THE TACO BOWLS

1½ cups water

1 cup long-grain white rice

1¼ pounds ground turkey

1 teaspoon sea salt

¼ teaspoon freshly ground black pepper

1 teaspoon ground coriander

½ teaspoon garlic powder

½ teaspoon ground cumin

½ teaspoon onion powder

¼ teaspoon dried oregano

¼ teaspoon paprika

1 (15-ounce) can black beans, drained and rinsed

1 cup frozen corn, thawed

Shredded lettuce, for topping

Diced tomato, for topping

Salsa, for topping

Avocado slices, for topping

Sliced olives, for topping

Shredded vegan cheese or Homemade Shredding Cheese (page 174), for topping

Lime wedges, for squeezing

## FOR THE GUACAMOLE

3 avocados, halved and pitted

2 tablespoons chopped fresh cilantro

Juice of 1 lime

Sea salt

Freshly ground black pepper

## TO MAKE THE TACO BOWLS

**1.** In a medium saucepan over high heat, bring the water to a boil. Pour in the rice and reduce the heat to low. Cover the pan and cook for about 20 minutes until the rice has absorbed all the water. Remove from the heat and let rest for 10 minutes.

**2.** Meanwhile, in a large skillet over medium-high heat, combine the ground turkey, salt, and pepper. Cook for 7 to 10 minutes, stirring to break up the meat, until the turkey is no longer pink.

**3.** Add the coriander, garlic powder, cumin, onion powder, oregano, paprika, black beans, and corn. Cook for 1 minute, stirring constantly. Turn the heat off and cover the skillet.

## TO MAKE THE GUACAMOLE AND ASSEMBLE THE BOWLS

**4.** Scoop the avocado flesh into a medium bowl. Add the cilantro and lime juice and mash together. Season with salt and pepper. Mash to your desired consistency.

**5.** To assemble the bowls, lay out 4 serving bowls. Put ¾ cup of rice in each bowl and top with one-fourth of the turkey. Let everyone add their favorite toppings.

**SIMPLIFY IT:** To save time, make the rice and the turkey filling up to 3 days ahead. Keep refrigerated in separate containers. Reheat in the microwave while you make the guacamole and prepare the toppings.

# VEGGIE-PACKED TURKEY MEAT LOAF WITH CORN ON THE COB

NUT-FREE

This is one of my all-time favorite recipes. It is a basic meat loaf with pureed fresh vegetables mixed into the meat, taking meat loaf to the next level. Chop any leftovers and add to spaghetti sauce, then serve over your favorite pasta for another meal.

**PREP TIME:**
20 MINUTES

**COOK TIME:**
50 MINUTES

**SERVES 4**

## FOR THE MEAT LOAF

Nonstick cooking spray

2 large eggs

½ white onion, roughly chopped

1 cup roughly chopped stemmed kale

2 large carrots, chopped

3 garlic cloves, peeled

¼ cup organic ketchup, plus more for topping

1 pound ground turkey

1 cup old-fashioned rolled oats

¼ cup nutritional yeast

1 tablespoon beef rub seasoning

¾ teaspoon sea salt

½ teaspoon freshly ground black pepper

## FOR THE CORN

4 ears fresh corn, husked and silks removed

Sea salt

Freshly ground black pepper

4 tablespoons (½ stick) vegan butter

## TO MAKE THE MEAT LOAF

**1.** Preheat the oven to 350°F. Lightly coat an 8½-by-4½-inch loaf pan with cooking spray.

**2.** In a food processor, combine the eggs, onion, kale, carrots, garlic, and ketchup. Process until smooth. Transfer the pureed vegetables into a large bowl and add the ground turkey, oats, nutritional yeast, beef rub seasoning, salt, and pepper. Using your clean hands, mix the ingredients until well combined and a little sticky. Put the mixture into the prepared loaf pan, spreading it evenly. Drizzle the top with ketchup.

**3.** Bake for 45 to 50 minutes, or until set.

## TO MAKE THE CORN

**4.** Tear off four sheets of aluminum foil large enough to wrap around each ear of corn. Place each cob on a foil sheet. Season with salt and pepper and top each ear with 1 tablespoon of butter. Wrap the foil around each ear.

**5.** After the meat loaf has cooked for 20 minutes, put the corn into the oven and cook until the meat loaf is done. Remove and serve the meat loaf with the corn on the side.

**RECIPE TIP:** Since the meat loaf has a slightly pink color from the carrots and ketchup, it can be tricky to tell if it is done. A meat thermometer should register 165°F.

*chapter nine*

# PORK AND BEEF

# SAUSAGE TORTILLA CUPS

Using tortillas makes this crust convenient and simple. Try switching up the recipe with beef or ground turkey for variation.

**PREP TIME:**
10 MINUTES

**COOK TIME:**
20 MINUTES

**SERVES 4
(3 TORTILLA
CUPS PER
SERVING)**

Nonstick cooking spray

3 (6-inch) corn tortillas, quartered

1 pound pork sausage

¾ cup mayonnaise

2 tablespoons yellow mustard

1 tablespoon nutritional yeast

½ cup finely chopped asparagus

½ red bell pepper, finely chopped

½ teaspoon onion powder

Sea salt

Freshly ground black pepper

1. Preheat the oven to 350°F. Lightly coat the interior of a 12-cup muffin tin with cooking spray.
2. Place each quarter tortilla into a muffin cup and press down with your hands so it sits inside the muffin cup and stays in.
3. Bake for 5 minutes until the edges begin to brown.
4. Meanwhile, in a large skillet over medium heat, cook the sausage for 7 to 10 minutes, stirring to break up the meat, until it is no longer pink. Drain and transfer to a large bowl.
5. Stir in the mayonnaise, mustard, nutritional yeast, asparagus, red bell pepper, and onion powder. Season with salt and pepper. Mix well. Scoop a rounded tablespoonful of the meat mixture into each tortilla cup.

**6.** Bake for 10 minutes or until heated through.

> **SERVING SUGGESTION:** Serve three on a plate with a simple side salad with Creamy Avocado Dressing (page 169) or with a side of Glazed Carrots (page 60).

# SPAGHETTI SQUASH ALFREDO WITH CRISPY BACON BITS

Kids love the noodle-y consistency of spaghetti squash and it's always a great way to incorporate healthy vegetables into a meal. Topping the noodles in a creamy sauce with salty, crispy bacon leaves everyone licking their bowls clean!

**PREP TIME:**
15 MINUTES

**COOK TIME:**
50 MINUTES

**SERVES 4**

1 (3-pound) spaghetti squash

2 tablespoons olive oil, divided

1 small shallot, minced

1 recipe Alfredo Sauce (page 171) or store-bought dairy-free Alfredo sauce

1 cup frozen peas, thawed

8 bacon slices, cooked and crumbled

1 teaspoon chopped fresh thyme leaves

Sea salt

Freshly ground black pepper

Chopped fresh parsley, for garnish

1. Preheat the oven to 400°F.
2. Halve the spaghetti squash lengthwise and discard the seeds and strings. Brush each half with 1½ teaspoons of oil and place each half, cut-side down, on a sheet pan. Add a splash of water to the bottom of the pan.
3. Roast for 45 minutes, or until the squash is tender when pierced with a fork. Set aside until cool enough to handle. Scrape the flesh with a fork and transfer the strands into a large bowl.
4. In a large saucepan over medium heat, heat the remaining 1 tablespoon of oil. Add the shallot and cook for 5 to 6 minutes, stirring often, or until soft. Add the Alfredo sauce. If the sauce is too thick, add water, 1 tablespoon at a time, until it reaches your desired consistency.

**5.** Add the warm squash "noodles," peas, bacon, and thyme and toss to combine. Season with salt and pepper to taste. Garnish with parsley.

**SUBSTITUTION TIP:** Add shredded cooked chicken for more meat, or to make it vegetarian and skip the meat, and add 1 (15-ounce) can cannellini beans, drained and rinsed, instead.

# SLOW COOKER BARBECUE SHREDDED PORK SLIDERS

EGG-FREE

Barbecue sauce is a close second to ketchup in the realm of kids' favorite sauces. Here, dinner practically makes itself. Just put all the ingredients into the slow cooker in the morning and by dinnertime you'll have sumptuous barbecue pork ready to eat.

**PREP TIME:**
10 MINUTES

**COOK TIME:**
6 TO 8 HOURS

**SERVES 8**

3 pounds pork tenderloin

½ cup chopped celery

2 cups organic ketchup

1 cup water

1 (5-ounce) bottle Worcestershire sauce

½ cup olive oil

¼ cup freshly squeezed lemon juice

¼ cup apple cider vinegar

¼ cup coconut sugar or dark brown sugar

1 tablespoon freshly ground black pepper

1 tablespoon ground mustard

Dash cayenne pepper

8 dairy-free slider buns or dinner rolls

1 cup baby arugula leaves or lettuce leaves

**1.** In a slow cooker, combine the pork tenderloin, celery, ketchup, water, Worcestershire sauce, oil, lemon juice, vinegar, coconut sugar, black pepper, mustard, and cayenne.

**2.** Cover the cooker and cook on Low heat for 6 to 8 hours.

**3.** Using two forks, twist to pull the pork into shreds. Serve on buns topped with arugula.

**LEFTOVERS:** Leftover barbecue pork is even more flavorful! Refrigerate leftovers in a sealed airtight container for up to 4 days. Serve in crunchy taco shells topped with fresh shredded cabbage, cilantro, and avocado slices.

# SHREDDED POTATO, HAM, AND BROCCOLI CASSEROLE

**GLUTEN-FREE**

I love serving my family casserole dishes that have loads of nutritional value in one dish while being easy for me to put together. The combination of eggs and milk creates a creamy thick texture a bit like ricotta.

**PREP TIME:**
15 MINUTES

**COOK TIME:**
45 MINUTES

**SERVES 4**

Nonstick cooking spray

1 tablespoon vegan butter

3 cups broccoli florets

½ cup chopped onion

2 garlic cloves, minced

1 tablespoon paprika

½ teaspoon sea salt

¼ teaspoon freshly ground black pepper

1 cup dairy-free milk

2 large eggs

1½ pounds Yukon Gold potatoes, grated

8 ounces cooked ham, cubed

1 tablespoon fresh rosemary leaves

1. Preheat the oven to 350°F. Lightly coat a 9-by-9-inch baking dish with cooking spray.
2. In a large saucepan over medium heat, melt the butter. Add the broccoli, onion, garlic, paprika, salt, and pepper. Cook for 5 minutes, or until the vegetables are slightly tender.
3. In a large bowl, whisk the milk and eggs. Stir in the potatoes, ham, and broccoli mixture. Transfer the casserole to the prepared baking dish.
4. Bake for 40 minutes, or until bubbly and slightly brown on top. Garnish with fresh rosemary and serve immediately.

**LEFTOVERS:** The leftovers are just as delicious as when first made. Cover and refrigerate for up to 3 days. To reheat, bake, covered, at 325°F for 20 minutes, or until warmed through.

# CORN DOG MUFFINS

A batter lightly sweetened with honey pairs perfectly with the salty hot dogs inside these muffins. Forget trying to make corn dogs on a stick; baking them in a muffin tin is less messy and they are just as enticing! My kids love these, as they can pick up the corn dog muffins and dip them in ketchup and mustard. Serve with steamed broccoli with a sprinkle of salt or fresh cucumber and carrot slices.

**PREP TIME:**
15 MINUTES

**COOK TIME:**
15 MINUTES

**MAKES 24 MINI MUFFINS (4 PER SERVING)**

Nonstick cooking spray

2 cups cornmeal

¾ cup all-purpose flour

1 teaspoon baking soda

½ teaspoon sea salt

2 large eggs

8 tablespoons (1 stick) vegan butter, at room temperature

⅓ cup honey

1 cup dairy-free milk, plus more as needed

½ cup dairy-free yogurt

6 beef or turkey hot dogs, quartered

Mustard, for serving

Organic ketchup, for serving

1. Preheat the oven to 400°F. Lightly coat the interior of a 24-cup mini muffin tin with cooking spray, or line it with mini paper muffin cups.
2. In a medium bowl, stir together the cornmeal, flour, baking soda, and salt.
3. In a large bowl, using an electric mixer on medium speed, beat together the eggs, butter, honey, milk, and yogurt until well mixed. Stir in the dry ingredients just until combined. The batter should be smooth. Add milk, 1 tablespoon at a time, to thin, if necessary. Spoon the batter into the prepared muffin cups.
4. Press 1 hot dog piece into the center of each muffin.

**5.** Bake for about 15 minutes until the tops are slightly golden.

**6.** Transfer the muffins to a wire cooling rack to cool completely. Serve with mustard and ketchup for dipping.

**LEFTOVERS:** Freeze leftovers for a speedy snack or meal. Make sure they are completely cool, then put them into a zip-top freezer bag and press out as much air as possible. Keep frozen for up to 2 months.

# TACO SALAD PIZZA WITH MAYO DRIZZLE

A meaty taco dinner just got a makeover served over pizza crust instead of in a taco shell. It is a combination of all-time-favorite kid foods—pizza and tacos—only without the cheese but still loads of flavor! We have been making this meal with all forms of ground meat and everyone loves it every time! I like to skip the cheese and serve it with this homemade creamy sauce, which adds a splash of zesty flavors. You can also top the pizza with salsa and Fresh Guacamole (page 118).

**PREP TIME:**
20 MINUTES

**COOK TIME:**
30 MINUTES

**MAKES
1 (12-INCH)
PIZZA**

**FOR THE MAYO DRIZZLE**
⅓ cup mayonnaise

1 tablespoon vegan butter, melted

2 teaspoons freshly squeezed lime juice

**FOR THE PIZZA**
Cassava flour, for dusting

1 recipe Grain-Free Flatbread dough (page 172), uncooked

2 tablespoons olive oil, divided

½ cup minced onion

1 pound ground beef

¾ cup tomato sauce

2 tablespoons mild taco seasoning

½ cup finely chopped butter lettuce

1 avocado, halved, pitted, peeled, and chopped

1 cup grape tomatoes, halved

1 tablespoon finely chopped fresh cilantro

**TO MAKE THE MAYO DRIZZLE**

**1.** In a small bowl, whisk the mayonnaise, melted butter, and lime juice to blend. Set aside.

## TO MAKE THE PIZZA

2. Preheat the oven to 500°F.

3. Lightly flour a piece of parchment paper. Form the dough into a disk and place it on the parchment. Using a rolling pin, roll the dough into a circle about 12 inches in diameter. Using the parchment paper, transfer the dough to a baking sheet.

4. Bake for 10 minutes. Remove the crust from the oven.

5. Meanwhile, in a large skillet over medium heat, heat 1 tablespoon of oil. Add the onion and cook for 5 minutes, or until it begins to soften.

6. Add the ground beef. Cook for 7 to 10 minutes, stirring to break up the meat, until it has browned. Stir in the tomato sauce and taco seasoning. Cook for 2 minutes. Turn off the heat.

7. Brush the remaining 1 tablespoon of oil over the crust. Spread the beef sauce over the crust and bake for 10 minutes, or until warm and the moisture has evaporated from the meat.

8. Top the pizza with lettuce, avocado, tomatoes, and cilantro and drizzle the sauce over the toppings. Slice and serve.

**SIMPLIFY IT:** To make this super easy, use a prebaked frozen store-bought dairy-free pizza crust. Thaw the crust, or top it and cook it right out of the freezer.

# GREEN BEAN AND BEEF RICE BOWLS

**EGG-FREE, NUT-FREE**

This is beautifully flavored with sauce made from soy, ginger, and vinegar with a touch of sugar that pairs well with steak. Serve it with extra soy sauce.

**PREP TIME:**
10 MINUTES

**COOK TIME:**
30 MINUTES,
PLUS
10 MINUTES
TO REST

**SERVES 4**

2 cups water

1⅓ cups long-grain white rice

1 pound boneless beef sirloin steak, cut into slices

Sea salt

Freshly ground black pepper

2 tablespoons olive oil

1 (15-ounce) can tomato sauce

¼ cup soy sauce

1 tablespoon apple cider vinegar

1 tablespoon light brown sugar

1 teaspoon garlic powder

½ teaspoon ground ginger

1 (14.5-ounce) can green beans, drained and rinsed

1. In a medium saucepan over high heat, bring the water to a boil. Pour in the rice and reduce the heat to low. Cover the pan and cook for about 20 minutes until the rice has absorbed all the water. Remove from the heat and let rest for 10 minutes.
2. While the rice rests, season the beef all over with salt and pepper.
3. In a large saucepan over medium-high heat, heat the oil. Carefully place the beef into the pan. Cook for 2 to 3 minutes until the meat is browned all over and juices are released.

4. Stir in the tomato sauce, soy sauce, vinegar, brown sugar, garlic powder, ginger, and green beans. Bring to a boil, then reduce the heat and simmer for 5 minutes. Serve over the cooked rice.

**SUBSTITUTION TIP:** If you prefer to use fresh green beans, simply cut off both ends, then cut the beans into thirds. Cover the bottom of a large skillet with water and add the green beans. Cover the skillet and bring to a boil over high heat. Reduce the heat to low and simmer the beans for 5 minutes, or until bright green. Add the beans to the recipe in step 4 as directed.

# SPAGHETTI SQUASH CHILI

**ALLERGEN-FREE, EGG-FREE, GLUTEN-FREE, NUT-FREE, SOY-FREE**

I love to use spaghetti squash in place of pasta noodles. It provides more vitamins, minerals, and fiber. Cook the squash in advance to have dinner on the table in about 30 minutes.

**PREP TIME:**
10 MINUTES

**COOK TIME:**
45 MINUTES

**SERVES 4**

1 (3-pound) spaghetti squash

2 tablespoons olive oil, divided

½ small white onion, finely chopped

2 garlic cloves, minced

1 pound ground beef

2 tablespoons tomato paste

2 teaspoons smoked paprika

1 teaspoon ground cumin

½ teaspoon dried oregano

1 teaspoon sea salt

½ teaspoon freshly ground pepper

2 (15-ounce) cans fire-roasted tomatoes with green chilies

1 cup water

1 (15-ounce) can kidney beans, drained and rinsed

1. Preheat the oven to 400°F.
2. Halve the spaghetti squash lengthwise and discard the seeds and strings. Brush each half with 1½ teaspoons of oil and place each half, cut-side down, on a sheet pan. Add a splash of water to the bottom of the pan.
3. Roast for 45 minutes, or until the squash is tender when pierced with a fork. Set aside until cool enough to handle. Scrape the flesh with a fork and transfer the strands into a large bowl.
4. Meanwhile, in a large saucepan over medium heat, heat the remaining 1 tablespoon of oil. Add the onion and garlic and cook for 3 minutes, stirring often.
5. Add the ground beef, tomato paste, paprika, cumin, oregano, salt, and pepper. Cook for 7 to 10 minutes, stirring to break up the meat, until the beef has browned.

**6.** Stir in the tomatoes and green chilies, water, and kidney beans. Bring the mixture to a boil, then reduce the heat to medium-low and simmer for 20 minutes.

**7.** Distribute the squash noodles among 4 plates and top with the chili.

**MAKE IT YOUR OWN:** Change the ingredients around by substituting conventional pasta for the spaghetti squash. Or use lean ground turkey in place of the beef for a dish lower in fat. For an additional pop of taste, add a sprinkle of nutritional yeast flakes on top.

# SLOPPY JOES

My siblings and I always loved sloppy joe night. This is a hearty meal with saucy meat and sweet and sour flavors that are a crowd-pleaser. Make a huge batch for a larger group or Super Bowl party by doubling or tripling the recipe and cooking it in a slow cooker.

**PREP TIME:**
15 MINUTES

**COOK TIME:**
45 MINUTES

**SERVES 6**

1 tablespoon olive oil

½ cup chopped sweet yellow onion

1 green bell pepper, finely chopped

2 pounds ground beef

1 cup organic ketchup

½ cup water

¼ cup finely chopped celery

1 tablespoon apple cider vinegar

1 tablespoon light brown sugar

1 tablespoon smoked paprika

1 tablespoon Dijon mustard

1½ teaspoons sea salt

1. In a large saucepan over medium-high heat, heat the oil. Add the onion and green bell pepper. Sauté for about 5 minutes, stirring constantly, or until the vegetables begin to soften.
2. Add the ground beef. Cook for 7 to 10 minutes, stirring to break up the meat, until it has browned. Drain any excess fat.
3. Stir in the ketchup, water, celery, vinegar, brown sugar, paprika, Dijon, and salt. Cover the pan, reduce the heat to low, and simmer for 30 minutes.

**4.** Serve in dairy-free rolls or in a bowl with a side of tortilla chips, if desired.

**SIMPLIFY IT:** Make this recipe In a slow cooker. Combine all the ingredients in a slow cooker, cover the cooker, and cook on Low heat for 4 hours. Stir a couple times as it cooks to break up the meat.

# SPEEDY SKILLET RIGATONI WITH MEAT SAUCE

The meat sauce is made with beef, but for a lighter dish, use lean ground turkey. I like to sneak in finely diced mushrooms for extra nutrition and earthy flavor.

**PREP TIME:**
15 MINUTES

**COOK TIME:**
25 MINUTES

**SERVES 4**

12 ounces dried rigatoni or ziti pasta

2 tablespoons olive oil

6 cremini mushrooms, finely diced

1 large carrot, grated

1 small white onion, diced

2 garlic cloves, diced

1 teaspoon dried oregano

1 pound ground beef

2 tablespoons red wine vinegar

1 tablespoon dried basil

1 (25-ounce) can crushed tomatoes

2 tablespoons tomato paste

1 teaspoon sea salt

¼ teaspoon freshly ground black pepper

**1.** Fill a large stockpot two-thirds full of water. Bring the water to a boil over high heat. Pour in the rigatoni and cook for 11 to 13 minutes, or until tender. Drain.

**2.** Meanwhile, in a large saucepan over medium heat, heat the oil. Add the mushrooms, carrot, onion, garlic, and oregano. Cook for about 5 minutes until the vegetables begin to soften.

**3.** Add the ground beef. Cook for 7 to 10 minutes, stirring to break up the meat, until it is lightly browned.

**4.** Add the vinegar and cook for 1 minute.

**5.** Stir in the basil, crushed tomatoes, and tomato paste and bring to a simmer, stirring often. Cook for 3 minutes. Season with salt and pepper and serve immediately over the rigatoni.

**SUBSTITUTION TIP:** If your family eats gluten-free, use gluten-free noodles.

# LASAGNA ROLL-UPS

This is a great family dinner that can be prepared up to 2 days ahead and baked right before serving. If you make it ahead, add an extra 5 to 10 minutes to the cooking time (25 to 30 minutes total).

**PREP TIME:**
15 MINUTES

**COOK TIME:**
40 MINUTES

**SERVES 4
(2 ROLL-UPS
PER
SERVING)**

1 (8-ounce) container vegan ricotta

2 large eggs

2 tablespoons chopped fresh basil

2 tablespoons chopped fresh parsley, plus more for garnish (optional)

8 lasagna noodles

2 tablespoons olive oil

1 small onion, diced

8 button mushrooms, finely diced

½ cup diced green bell pepper

2 garlic cloves, minced

1½ pounds ground beef

1 (24-ounce) jar marinara sauce

Nonstick cooking spray

Nutritional yeast, for garnish (optional)

1. In a small bowl, whisk the ricotta, eggs, basil, and parsley to combine. Cover and refrigerate until ready to use.
2. Fill a large stockpot two-thirds full of water. Bring the water to a boil over high heat. Slide the lasagna noodles into the water and cook for 11 to 12 minutes, or until al dente. Drain the noodles and rinse them with cold water. Lay each noodle flat on a sheet of aluminum foil or parchment paper.
3. Meanwhile, in a large saucepan over medium heat, heat the oil. Add the onion, mushrooms, green bell pepper, and garlic. Sauté for about 5 minutes, or until the vegetables are tender. Transfer the vegetables to a medium bowl.
4. Return the pan to medium heat and add the ground beef. Cook for 7 to 10 minutes, stirring to break up the meat, or until browned and cooked through. Add the cooked vegetables to the meat, pour in the marinara sauce, and stir to combine.

5. Preheat the oven to 375°F. Lightly coat a 9-by-9-inch baking dish with cooking spray.

6. Spread a thin layer of meat sauce on the bottom of the prepared pan.

7. Spread 2 tablespoons of the ricotta filling over each lasagna noodle, then roll up the noodles. Lay each roll seam-side down in the pan. Pour the remaining meat sauce over the top of the lasagna rolls.

8. Bake for 20 minutes until hot and bubbly. Top with nutritional yeast and chopped parsley (if using).

**LEFTOVERS:** Keep any leftovers refrigerated in an airtight container for up to 3 days. To reheat, return to a baking dish, cover with foil and bake at 325°F for about 25 minutes until warmed.

# SKIRT STEAK WITH ROASTED ASPARAGUS AND FINGERLING POTATOES

**EGG-FREE, NUT-FREE**

This meal of tender steak with crisp asparagus and roasted fingerling potatoes is a classic and will quickly become a family favorite. Fingerling potatoes
are small oblong potatoes that have a soft, buttery texture. Because of their
size, they cook quickly and are perfect for nights when you crave potatoes
but need to get dinner on the table quickly.

**PREP TIME:**
20 MINUTES

**COOK TIME:**
30 MINUTES

**SERVES 4**

1 pound asparagus,
woody ends removed,
cut into 1-inch pieces

5 tablespoons avocado
oil, divided

Sea salt

Freshly ground
black pepper

1 pound fingerling
potatoes, cut into thirds

1 pound skirt steak

2 garlic cloves, minced

2 tablespoons soy sauce

1 tablespoon minced
peeled fresh ginger

1. Preheat the oven to 400°F. Line a baking sheet with
parchment paper.

2. Put the asparagus in a small bowl. Drizzle 2½ tablespoons
of oil over the asparagus and season with salt and pepper
to taste. Toss to coat the asparagus in the oil and seasoning.

3. Put the potatoes on the prepared baking sheet. Drizzle
2½ tablespoons of oil over the potatoes and season with
salt and pepper to taste. Toss to coat the potatoes in the oil
and seasoning. On half of the baking sheet, spread the potatoes into a single layer, leaving the other half empty (you will
add the asparagus to that side later).

4. Bake the potatoes for 20 minutes.

5. Once the potatoes have baked for 10 minutes, start
the steak. Season the steak all over with salt and pepper.
Set aside.

**6.** In a large skillet over high heat, heat the remaining 1 tablespoon of oil. Add the garlic, soy sauce, and ginger. Cook for 30 seconds, or until fragrant. Add the steak and cook for 8 to 9 minutes, turning once, or until it reaches an internal temperature of 145°F. Transfer the steak to a cutting board, cover it with aluminum foil, and let rest for 10 minutes.

**7.** Once you've transferred the steak to a cutting board and covered it (this should be about the time your potatoes have baked for 20 minutes), flip the potatoes, add the asparagus to the pan, and roast for 10 minutes more.

**8.** Cut the steak into slices and serve it with the roasted asparagus and potatoes.

**MAKE IT YOUR OWN:** There are many possible variations on this dish. You can use any cut of steak you like including flank steak, rib eye, or New York strip. You could also use this preparation for pork chops. Just adjust the cooking time according to the thickness of the meat and remember it should reach an internal temperature of 145°F.

# SLOW COOKER BEEF STEW

**EGG-FREE, NUT-FREE, SOY-FREE**

Cozying up indoors with a hearty bowl of beef stew is household bliss. Tender chunks of beef, potatoes, and carrots are slowly cooked to melt in your mouth with every bite. This is a great recipe to have on hand and leftovers taste even better as the flavors settle. Make it in the morning or on the weekends and have it ready when you are.

**PREP TIME:**
20 MINUTES

**COOK TIME:**
4 TO 6 HOURS

**SERVES 4**

½ cup all-purpose flour

½ teaspoon sea salt

2 tablespoons olive oil

1 large shallot, minced

2 pounds beef stew meat

1 teaspoon dried thyme

½ teaspoon dried oregano

1 bay leaf

3 cups low-sodium beef broth

2 cups tomato sauce

1½ pounds (about 8 small) Yukon Gold potatoes, quartered

8 ounces carrots, cut into 1-inch-thick slices

1. In a large bowl, stir together the flour and salt until well combined.
2. In a large skillet over medium-high heat, heat the oil. Add the shallot and cook for about 2 minutes to soften. Transfer the shallot to the slow cooker. Return the skillet to the heat.
3. Put the stew meat in the flour mixture and toss to coat. Shake off excess flour and add the meat in the skillet, spacing the pieces out so they brown, not steam. Cook for 3 to 4 minutes per side to brown. (Depending on the size of your skillet, you may have to do this in batches.) Transfer the meat to the slow cooker.
4. Add the thyme, oregano, bay leaf, beef broth, tomato sauce, potatoes, and carrots.

**5.** Cover the cooker and cook on Low heat for 4 to 6 hours, or until the beef and vegetables are tender.

**6.** Refrigerate leftovers in an airtight container for up to 3 days.

**SERVING SUGGESTION:** Serve this stew over egg noodles or with Creamy Mashed Cauliflower (page 62).

*chapter ten*

# DESESERTS

# STRAWBERRY YOGURT ICE POPS

**EGG-FREE, GLUTEN-FREE, VEGETARIAN**

My kids' favorite frozen treats are the packaged strawberry yogurt sticks from our favorite grocery stores. These taste just like them and are quickly made at home without the use of dairy. It is a healthy treat, full of vitamin C and probiotics.

**PREP TIME:**
10 MINUTES,
PLUS 8 HOURS
TO FREEZE

**MAKES 6 ICE
POPS**

2 cups dairy-free
vanilla yogurt

½ cup Cashew Milk
(page 22) or store-bought
cashew milk

2 cups fresh
strawberries, hulled

2 tablespoons honey

→ In a high-speed blender, combine the yogurt, milk, strawberries, and honey. Blend on high speed until smooth. Pour into 6 ice pop molds. Freeze for 8 hours, or overnight.

**MAKE IT YOUR OWN:** Change up this recipe using 2 cups blueberries for blue ice pops or 1½ cups chopped kiwi and ½ cup fresh spinach for green ice pops.

# NO-CHURN VANILLA ICE CREAM

GLUTEN-FREE, SOY-FREE, VEGETARIAN

Although this ice cream does not require churning, you can make it in an ice-cream maker, if you have one. To do so, skip step 3 and freeze the custard in your ice-cream maker according to the manufacturer's instructions.

**PREP TIME:**
5 MINUTES,
PLUS 8 HOURS
TO FREEZE

**COOK TIME:**
11 MINUTES

**MAKES
4 CUPS**

2 (13.5-ounce) cans coconut milk

½ cup organic cane sugar

3 large egg yolks

1 tablespoon freshly squeezed lemon juice

1 teaspoon vanilla extract

1. In a large saucepan over low heat, warm the coconut milk for 5 minutes.
2. Add the sugar, egg yolks, lemon juice, and vanilla. Increase the heat to medium-low and cook the custard, whisking constantly, for about 6 minutes, or until hot and thickened. Do not boil. Remove from the heat and transfer to a glass container. Let cool.
3. Cover the container and place the custard in the freezer. Stir every 30 minutes for 2 hours, then freeze for 4 to 6 hours more (6 to 8 hours total) until firm.
4. When ready to serve, let sit at room temperature for 10 to 15 minutes until soft enough to scoop.

**SERVING SUGGESTION:** For an extra-special treat, set up a sundae bar with this ice cream, Chocolate-Chocolate Chip Ice Cream (page 152); Caramel Sauce (page 167); Whipped Cream (page 166); and your favorite fruit, nut, or candy toppings.

# CHOCOLATE-CHOCOLATE CHIP ICE CREAM

**EGG-FREE, GLUTEN-FREE, SOY-FREE, VEGAN**

Rich vegan chocolate chip ice cream is a breeze with this simple no-cook method. Although this ice cream does not require churning, you can make it in an ice-cream maker, if you have one. To do so, skip step 2 and freeze in your ice-cream maker according to the manufacturer's instructions. Serve with warm Best Fudgy Brownies Ever (page 156) or your favorite toppings.

**PREP TIME:**
5 MINUTES,
PLUS 8 HOURS
TO FREEZE

**MAKES
3 CUPS**

1 (13.5-ounce) can coconut milk or coconut cream

½ cup cocoa powder

⅓ cup maple syrup

1 teaspoon vanilla extract

¼ cup dairy-free mini chocolate chips

1. In a high-speed blender, combine the coconut milk, cocoa powder, maple syrup, and vanilla. Blend until smooth, then transfer to a freezer-safe dish. Sprinkle with chocolate chips.
2. Cover the container and place it in the freezer. Stir every 30 minutes for 2 hours. Then freeze for 4 to 6 hours more (6 to 8 hours total) until firm.
3. When ready to serve, let sit at room temperature for 10 to 15 minutes until soft enough to scoop.

**MAKE IT YOUR OWN:** This basic recipe can be made into a variety of flavors. Instead of cocoa powder, use dried strawberries or dried blueberries blended into a powder for a fruity option.

# CHUNKY OAT COOKIES

**EGG-FREE, VEGETARIAN**

These cookies are packed with wholesome ingredients, not to mention chunky and scrumptious with coconut and chocolate flavors! If your child is not a fan of dried fruit, swap the raisins for more chocolate chips. Serve these cookies for dessert or as an afternoon treat.

**PREP TIME:**
15 MINUTES

**COOK TIME:**
15 MINUTES,
PLUS
10 MINUTES
TO COOL

**MAKES
15 COOKIES**

8 tablespoons
(1 stick) vegan butter,
at room temperature

¼ cup honey

1 teaspoon vanilla extract

½ teaspoon baking soda

¾ cup whole-wheat flour

1 cup quick-cooking oats

1 cup fine unsweetened macaroon coconut (such as Bob's Red Mill brand)

½ cup pumpkin seeds

¼ cup dairy-free dark chocolate chips

½ cup organic cane sugar

¼ cup raisins

½ teaspoon
ground cinnamon

1. Preheat the oven to 350°F. Line 2 baking sheets with parchment paper.
2. In a large bowl, using an electric mixer on medium speed, beat the butter, honey, vanilla, and baking soda for 1 minute.
3. Add the flour, oats, coconut, pumpkin seeds, chocolate chips, sugar, raisins, and cinnamon. Mix on low speed for 3 minutes, or until combined.
4. Roll the dough into 15 balls and place them on the prepared baking sheets about 2 inches apart. Wet your hands to prevent sticking and press each ball down.
5. Bake for about 15 minutes, or until golden brown. Let cool on the baking sheets for 10 minutes, then transfer to a wire cooling rack to cool completely.

# CHOCOLATE CHUNK MARSHMALLOW BARS

Enjoy these buttery blondie bars at all of your favorite celebrations. When served warm the chocolate and marshmallow will be wonderfully gooey. I share this recipe at the suggestion of my youngest. He loves to add marshmallows into just about every baked good and wants to share this recipe with kids "around the world."

**PREP TIME:**
15 MINUTES

**COOK TIME:**
25 MINUTES

**MAKES**
**24 SQUARES**

1 cup (2 sticks) vegan butter, melted

⅔ cup organic cane sugar

⅔ cup packed light brown sugar

2 teaspoons vanilla extract

3 large eggs

2 cups all-purpose flour

1 cup quick-cooking oats

1 teaspoon salt

1 teaspoon baking powder

½ teaspoon baking soda

1½ cups dairy-free dark chocolate chips

1½ cups mini marshmallows

1. Preheat the oven to 350°F. Line a 9-by-13-inch baking dish with parchment paper (so it covers the bottom and comes up the sides).
2. In a large bowl, using an electric mixer on medium speed, cream together the melted butter, cane sugar, brown sugar, vanilla, and eggs.
3. Using a rubber spatula, stir in the flour, oats, salt, baking powder, and baking soda.
4. Fold in the chocolate chips and marshmallows. Spread the mixture into the prepared pan in an even layer.

**5.** Bake for 20 to 25 minutes, or until golden brown. Set the pan on a wire cooling rack to cool. While still warm, but cool enough to handle, cut the bars into squares and serve.

**DID YOU KNOW?** Did you know marshmallows are dairy free? If you thought they contained dairy, you are not alone. Natural marshmallows are typically made of tapioca flour, tapioca sugar, and gelatin, which make them white and fluffy without milk products.

# BEST FUDGY BROWNIES EVER

Extra fudgy chocolate brownies with a creamy filling that simply melts in your mouth! These take little time to whip up and are a crowd-pleaser. Make sure to bake the brownies in the upper third of the oven for no longer than 25 minutes for the best consistency.

**PREP TIME:**
15 MINUTES

**COOK TIME:**
25 MINUTES, PLUS 2 HOURS TO COOL

**MAKES 16 BROWNIES**

1¼ cups dairy-free chocolate chunks or dairy-free chocolate chips, melted

1 cup coconut oil, melted

5 large eggs

2 cups coconut sugar or packed light brown sugar

1 tablespoon vanilla extract

1 cup all-purpose flour

¼ cup unsweetened cocoa powder

½ teaspoon sea salt

1. Place an oven rack in the upper third of the oven and pre-heat the oven to 375°F. Line a 9-by-9-inch baking pan with parchment paper.

2. In a medium microwave-safe bowl, combine the chocolate chunks and oil. Microwave on high power for 1 to 2 minutes, stirring every 30 seconds, until the mixture starts to melt. Stir to melt completely.

3. In a large bowl, using an electric mixer on high speed, beat the eggs, coconut sugar, and vanilla for about 10 minutes until light in color and thick. Reduce the speed to low and beat in the melted chocolate.

4. Slowly add the flour, cocoa powder, and salt and mix, stopping to scrape down the sides and bottom of the bowl as needed, just until blended. Pour the batter into the pre-pared baking pan.

5. Bake for about 25 minutes until the edges are slightly cracked and a toothpick inserted into the center comes out with moist crumbs. Do not overbake.

**6.** Let cool for 10 minutes, then use the parchment paper to lift the brownies from the baking pan. Cool on a wire cooling rack for 2 hours before cutting.

**LEFTOVERS:** Store the brownies in an airtight container at room temperature for up to 3 days, or refrigerate for 5 to 7 days. To freeze, line aluminum foil with wax paper. Tightly wrap the brownies in the wax paper and aluminum foil and put them into a zip-top freezer bag. Freeze for up to 3 months. Thaw before eating.

# VANILLA CUPCAKES WITH BUTTERCREAM ICING

VEGETARIAN

Thanks to yogurt and applesauce, kids can indulge in a lighter, healthier cupcake for parties and everyday celebrations! These cupcakes have a buttercream frosting using whipped vegan butter, confectioners' sugar, and a splash of vanilla. If using plain sugar, these cupcakes will be lighter in color as coconut sugar lends a darker color.

**PREP TIME:**
15 MINUTES

**COOK TIME:**
20 MINUTES

**MAKES
12 ICED
CUPCAKES**

### FOR THE CUPCAKES
1 cup coconut sugar or organic cane sugar

1¼ cups dairy-free plain yogurt

½ cup avocado oil

2 large eggs

1 teaspoon vanilla extract

2 cups whole-wheat flour or all-purpose flour

1½ teaspoons baking powder

½ teaspoon baking soda

½ teaspoon salt

### FOR THE ICING
1 cup (2 sticks) vegan butter, at room temperature

¼ to ½ cup unsweetened dairy-free milk

1 tablespoon vanilla extract

5 cups confectioners' sugar

### TO MAKE THE CUPCAKES
1. Preheat the oven to 350°F. Line a 12-cup muffin tin with paper cupcake liners.
2. In a large bowl, whisk the coconut sugar, yogurt, oil, eggs, and vanilla until blended.
3. In another large bowl, stir together the flour, baking powder, baking soda, and salt. Pour the wet ingredients into the dry ingredients. Using a rubber spatula, combine the ingredients to form a batter. Evenly divide the batter among the prepared muffin cups.

**4.** Bake for 18 to 20 minutes, or until slightly golden and a toothpick inserted into the center of a cupcake comes out clean. Cool for 5 minutes in the pan, then transfer to a wire cooling rack to cool completely.

## TO MAKE THE ICING

**5.** In a large bowl, using an electric mixer on high speed, beat the butter, ¼ cup of milk, and the vanilla until smooth.

**6.** Beat in the confectioners' sugar until the icing is smooth and spreadable, adding more milk, 1 tablespoon at a time, to achieve the right consistency.

**7.** When the cupcakes are completely cool, spread or pipe the icing over the top.

**SIMPLIFY IT:** The icing can be made in advance and kept refrigerated for up to 1 week. When ready to use, let it come to room temperature, then whip until fluffy. Spread with a knife, or add to a piping bag and ice the cupcakes with designs.

# CHOCOLATE BIRTHDAY CAKE WITH CHOCOLATE GANACHE ICING

**VEGETARIAN**

Just because you can't have dairy should never mean you can't enjoy a yummy chocolaty birthday cake. This cake is incredibly moist and full of chocolate flavor. It's topped with a fudgy whipped ganache icing that takes just moments to make.

**PREP TIME:**
25 MINUTES

**COOK TIME:**
25 MINUTES

**SERVES 12**

## FOR THE CAKE

Nonstick cooking spray

2 cups all-purpose flour

1 cup cocoa powder

1 tablespoon baking powder

1 teaspoon baking soda

1 teaspoon sea salt

6 tablespoons (¾ stick) vegan butter, at room temperature

1½ cups packed light brown sugar

¼ cup maple syrup

5 large eggs

1 cup dairy-free plain yogurt

2 teaspoons apple cider vinegar

2 teaspoons vanilla extract

## FOR THE CHOCOLATE GANACHE ICING

3 cups dairy-free dark chocolate chips

2 cups coconut cream

2 teaspoons vanilla extract

## TO MAKE THE CAKE

**1.** Preheat the oven to 350°F. Lightly coat 3 (9-inch) round cake pans with cooking spray.

**2.** In a medium bowl, stir together the flour, cocoa, baking powder, baking soda, and salt.

**3.** In a large bowl, using an electric mixer on medium speed, cream together the butter, brown sugar, and maple syrup for about 3 minutes until fluffy. Reduce the speed to low and beat in the eggs, yogurt, vinegar, and vanilla until combined, stopping to scrape down the sides of the bowl, as needed.

**4.** Slowly add the dry ingredients to the wet ingredients and mix until incorporated. Evenly divide the batter among the prepared pans.

**5.** Bake for 20 to 25 minutes, or until a toothpick inserted into the center comes out clean.

**6.** Let cool for 15 minutes, then carefully remove the cakes from the pans and transfer to a wire cooling rack to cool completely.

## TO MAKE THE CHOCOLATE GANACHE ICING

**7.** Place the chocolate chips in a large heatproof bowl.

**8.** In a small saucepan over medium-high heat, heat the coconut cream for 2 to 3 minutes until it is just about to boil. Remove the pan from the heat and pour the hot coconut cream over the chocolate chips. Whisk until melted and combined. Add the vanilla.

**9.** Using an electric mixer on medium speed, mix for about 3 minutes until very smooth and creamy.

**10.** When the cake is completely cooled, spread the icing between the layers, over the top, and around the sides.

> **DID YOU KNOW?** Cakes are great to make in advance, then prepare and decorate right before a big event. They can be made a day ahead and refrigerated, or can be frozen in an airtight zip-top freezer bag for up to 2 months. The ganache can be made up to 1 week in advance and kept refrigerated in an airtight container.

# CHOCOLATE CHIP CARAMEL BREAD PUDDING

**SOY-FREE, VEGETARIAN**

Kids like anything with chocolate and, when you mix it with creamy caramel and serve it to them in this bread pudding, they will be dancing with joy for days. This pudding is perfect for holiday gatherings or for brunch served with fresh berries.

**PREP TIME:**
15 MINUTES, PLUS
20 MINUTES TO SOAK

**COOK TIME:**
45 MINUTES

**SERVES 10**

Nonstick cooking spray

6 large eggs

1 (13-ounce) can coconut cream

¾ cup Caramel Sauce (page 167), divided

¾ cup dairy-free mini chocolate chips

½ cup chopped pecans

1 teaspoon ground cinnamon

1 teaspoon vanilla extract

1 loaf dairy-free bread, cubed

1. Lightly coat a 9-by-9-inch baking dish with cooking spray.
2. In a large bowl, whisk the eggs, coconut cream, ½ cup of caramel sauce, the chocolate chips, pecans, cinnamon, and vanilla until blended. Add the bread and gently stir until the bread is coated in the sauce. Transfer the pudding to the prepared baking dish. Cover and let soak for 20 minutes.
3. About 10 minutes before the bread is done soaking, preheat the oven to 375°F.
4. Bake the pudding, covered, for 30 minutes. Uncover the dish and bake for 15 minutes more, or until the top is golden brown. Drizzle with the remaining ¼ cup of caramel sauce before serving.

**SIMPLIFY IT:** Use chocolate chip bread instead of adding chocolate chips. Also, if your child doesn't care for nuts, leave them out.

# HOMEMADE MINI PEANUT BUTTER CUPS

**EGG-FREE, GLUTEN-FREE, VEGAN**

For children who cannot eat candy or chocolate due to a dairy intolerance, this is a wonderful treat. I like to make these cups at night while the kids sleep, otherwise they want to eat them all in one sitting. These treats are great for Easter, to serve at holiday gatherings, or as dessert when kids eat all their dinner.

**PREP TIME:**
20 MINUTES,
PLUS 1 HOUR
30 MINUTES
TO CHILL

**COOK TIME:**
2 MINUTES

**MAKES
24 MINI
PEANUT
BUTTER
CUPS**

⅔ cup organic peanut butter

¼ cup confectioners' sugar

4 tablespoons (½ stick) vegan butter, at room temperature

2¼ cups dairy-free chocolate chunks

1. Line a 24-cup mini muffin tin with paper cupcake liners.
2. In a medium bowl, stir together the peanut butter, confectioners' sugar, and butter. Cover and chill for 30 minutes.
3. Put the chocolate in a medium microwave bowl and microwave on high power for 30 seconds, then stir. Heat in 30-second intervals, stirring between each, until the chocolate melts.
4. Using a teaspoon, put 1 teaspoon of chocolate into the bottom of each muffin liner. Scoop 1 teaspoon of the peanut butter mixture into each cup and press it down so the chocolate goes up the sides. Top each peanut butter cup with another teaspoon of melted chocolate.
5. Chill for 1 hour to harden.
6. Wrap in candy wrappers to enjoy as treats, or store in a sealed container in a cool dry place for up to 3 weeks.

**SUBSTITUTION TIP:** Any nut butter or seed butter can be used, such as cashew butter, almond butter, or sunflower seed butter.

*chapter eleven*

# STAPLES, SAUCES, DRESSINGS

# WHIPPED CREAM

A light, fluffy topping for ice-cream sundaes, angel food cakes, pancakes, or even stirred into oatmeal in the morning for a festive weekday breakfast treat, this coconut-based whipped cream whips up in minutes, or make it ahead and keep refrigerated in an airtight container for up to 5 days. Make sure the coconut cream is chilled before starting.

**PREP TIME:**
6 MINUTES, AFTER CHILLING THE COCONUT CREAM FOR 24 HOURS

**MAKES 1½ CUPS**

1 (13.5-ounce) can coconut cream, chilled for 24 hours

½ cup confectioners' sugar

½ teaspoon vanilla extract

1. Turn the can of coconut cream upside down and open it. Scoop the solid cream into a large bowl. Reserve the liquid for another recipe, such as a smoothie.
2. Using an electric mixer on high speed, beat the cream for about 5 minutes until it has the consistency of whipped cream. Add the confectioners' sugar and vanilla and beat for 1 minute more until blended.

**MAKE IT YOUR OWN:** Use almond extract, orange extract, peppermint extract, or lemon extract instead of vanilla.

# CARAMEL SAUCE

Caramel is one of my kids' favorite sugary treats to put on top of ice cream and dessert. The only problem is, it is typically made with dairy. My kids love this version just as much (if not more) than the store-bought version, and I can make it in 30 minutes or less. Store it in the refrigerator so it's at the ready anytime you need a rich and creamy caramel sauce for desserts.

**PREP TIME:**
5 MINUTES

**COOK TIME:**
20 MINUTES,
PLUS
10 MINUTES
TO COOL

**MAKES
2 CUPS**

1 cup coconut cream

1 cup coconut sugar or dark brown sugar

4 tablespoons (½ stick) vegan butter

1 teaspoon vanilla extract

Pinch sea salt

1. In a small pot over high heat, combine the coconut cream, coconut sugar, butter, vanilla, and salt. Bring to a boil, whisking while the butter melts. When the caramel starts to boil around the edges, immediately turn the heat to low so the caramel does not burn. Simmer for 15 minutes, whisking constantly.

2. Let cool for 10 minutes to thicken and transfer to a glass container, cover, and refrigerate for up to 4 days.

**DID YOU KNOW?** If you are not going to use all the caramel sauce, freeze it in an airtight container and use within 2 months.

# HONEY MUSTARD SAUCE

GLUTEN-FREE, NUT-FREE, SOY-FREE, VEGETARIAN

Kids love this dip. It goes great with pretty much everything. Use this for nuggets, sandwiches, with meats, and as a spread.

**PREP TIME:**
5 MINUTES

**MAKES**
1¾ CUPS

1 cup mayonnaise

2 tablespoons Dijon mustard

2 tablespoons yellow mustard

½ cup honey

2 teaspoons apple cider vinegar

Sea salt

Freshly ground black pepper

→ In a small bowl, whisk the mayonnaise, Dijon, yellow mustard, honey, and vinegar to blend. Season with salt and pepper to taste and whisk again. Refrigerate in an airtight container for up to 4 weeks.

**SUBSTITUTION TIP:** To make this vegan, use vegan mayonnaise and maple syrup instead of honey. Or change up the flavors by adding 2 tablespoons ketchup to the mix.

# CREAMY AVOCADO DRESSING

**GLUTEN-FREE, VEGETARIAN**

A creamy dressing ready at a moment's notice when you need a drizzle of cream where cheese would be. Top taco dishes, meats, and roasted vegetables with this sauce for some zesty flavor.

**PREP TIME:**
10 MINUTES

**MAKES
2½ CUPS**

1 avocado, halved and pitted

¼ cup dairy-free plain yogurt

¼ cup mayonnaise

1 cup water

1 cup fresh cilantro leaves with stems or basil leaves

Juice of ½ lime

1 large garlic clove, peeled

½ teaspoon sea salt

→ Scoop the avocado flesh into a high-speed blender and add the yogurt, mayonnaise, water, cilantro, lime juice, garlic, and salt. Blend on high speed until smooth. Transfer to an airtight container and refrigerate until ready to use. Use within 1 day.

**MAKE IT YOUR OWN:** Serving an Italian feast? Use fresh basil and parsley in place of cilantro. Get creative with the herbs. If serving seafood, replace the cilantro with a dill and basil blend.

# QUESO DIPPING CHEESE

**EGG-FREE, GLUTEN-FREE, SOY-FREE, VEGAN**

This mellow dip shines accompanied by tortilla chips, or as a cheese sauce for any number of dishes. It is made from cashews soaked in water for a long time, which gives this dip its rich, creamy texture.

**PREP TIME:**
5 MINUTES,
PLUS
8 HOURS, OR
OVERNIGHT,
TO SOAK

**MAKES
1½ CUPS**

1½ cups raw unsalted cashews

1 cup filtered water, plus more as needed

¼ cup nutritional yeast

1 tablespoon freshly squeezed lemon juice

½ teaspoon garlic powder

½ teaspoon sea salt

½ teaspoon ground cumin

Pinch ground turmeric

1. In a medium bowl, combine the cashews and water. Let soak for 8 hours, or overnight. Drain the water and rinse the cashews.

2. In a high-speed blender, combine the soaked cashews, nutritional yeast, lemon juice, garlic powder, salt, cumin, and turmeric. Blend on high speed until very smooth. The consistency should be fairly thick but thin enough to drizzle over chips, salads, or vegetables. Add water, a bit at a time, if needed for your desired consistency. Refrigerate in an airtight container for up to 3 days

**SUBSTITUTION TIP:** Blanched, unsalted almonds, without skins, can be substituted for the cashews in the same amount.

# ALFREDO SAUCE

A creamy delicate sauce made without dairy! This simple sauce can be used for anything calling for savory canned cream soup, including green beans, tossed over pasta, or in a casserole. It is bursting with earthy flavor and buttery taste.

**PREP TIME:**
5 MINUTES

**COOK TIME:**
10 MINUTES

**MAKES**
**2¾ CUPS**

3 tablespoons vegan butter

½ teaspoon salt

½ teaspoon onion powder

½ teaspoon garlic powder

3 tablespoons all-purpose flour

⅔ cup coconut milk, chilled

⅔ cup low-sodium chicken broth, chilled

1 tablespoon nutritional yeast

1. In a large saucepan over medium heat, melt the butter. Whisk in the salt, onion powder, and garlic powder.
2. Slowly whisk in the flour and cook, whisking, for 1 minute.
3. Turn the heat to low, then add the chilled coconut milk, chicken broth, and nutritional yeast. Cook for about 1 minute, whisking, until warmed and slightly thickened.
4. Serve immediately, or refrigerate in an airtight container for up to 4 days.

**SUBSTITUTION TIP:** Adding canned coconut milk works best to create the most flavorful creamy sauce. It can be substituted with unsweetened almond milk, but the sauce will not get quite as thick and creamy.

# GRAIN-FREE FLATBREAD

**EGG-FREE, GLUTEN-FREE, VEGAN**

This is a fast way to enjoy grain-free pizza crust. The bread can also be used as a base for sandwiches or folded over like a pita. This dough will yield four small crusts, or you can bake it as one large 12-inch crust. You can also double the recipe to make two large crusts or eight small crusts.

**PREP TIME:**
15 MINUTES

**COOK TIME:**
20 MINUTES

**MAKES
4 SMALL
FLATBREADS**

1¼ cups plain dairy-free yogurt

2 tablespoons extra virgin olive oil

1 teaspoon apple cider vinegar

5 tablespoons of water, divided

1 cup cassava flour, plus more for the work surface

¼ cup arrowroot flour

2 tablespoons flaxseed meal

1 tablespoon baking powder

¾ teaspoon sea salt

¼ teaspoon baking soda

1. Preheat the oven to 500°F. Line a baking sheet with parchment paper.

2. In a large bowl, whisk the yogurt, oil, vinegar, and 4 tablespoons of water to blend.

3. Add the cassava and arrowroot flours, flaxseed meal, baking powder, salt, and baking soda. Using a rubber spatula, stir until a dough forms. If needed, add 1 more tablespoon of water. The dough will be sticky but should form a dough ball.

4. Dust a clean work surface with cassava flour. Using your clean hands, roll the dough into a ball and flatten it into a disk, or divide the dough into 4 disks. Press the dough flat with your hands, then, using a rolling pin, roll out one disk to a 12-inch crust, or 4 small crusts, each to about ¼ inch thick. Transfer the crust(s) to the prepared baking sheet.

**5.** Bake for 10 minutes.

**6.** For pizza, top the crust with your preferred toppings and bake for 5 to 7 minutes more.

**7.** Freeze the cooked crusts in an airtight zip-top bag for up to 1 month.

**DID YOU KNOW?** Flaxseed meal adds fiber and healthy brain-boosting omega-3 fatty acids to your diet. Adding it to grain-free breads using cassava flour helps the ingredients bind and stay moist.

# HOMEMADE SHREDDING CHEESE

EGG-FREE, GLUTEN-FREE, SOY-FREE, VEGAN

This recipe offers a simple way to enjoy shredded and melted cheese while still avoiding dairy. My family is not a fan of most store-bought vegan cheeses, as their flavor can be overwhelming. I created this version for you if your family is the same way. Use it in sandwiches, burritos, tacos, and over pizza. It has a nice, mild cheese-like flavor with a slightly crumbly texture.

**PREP TIME:**
5 MINUTES

**COOK TIME:**
5 MINUTES,
PLUS 8 HOURS
TO CHILL

**MAKES
ABOUT
1½ CUPS**

3 tablespoons refined coconut oil

¾ teaspoon sea salt

½ cup potato starch

1 cup almond milk

2 teaspoons apple cider vinegar

1 teaspoon nutritional yeast

1 teaspoon freshly squeezed lemon juice

¼ teaspoon baking soda

1. In a medium saucepan over medium heat, melt the coconut oil. Add the salt and potato starch and cook, stirring constantly, for 2 minutes, or until the mixture starts to thin. (Be careful not to burn it!) Reduce the heat to low. (It will become very thick, with a paste-like consistency as it heats.)
2. Pour in the milk, vinegar, nutritional yeast, lemon juice, and baking soda. Mix to form a dough. It will thicken, so use a rubber spatula. Turn off the heat.
3. Transfer the cheese to a sheet of plastic wrap. Wrap up the cheese and chill for 8 hours. Slice or shred the cheese for serving.

**MAKE IT YOUR OWN:** If you want to make the cheese more solid and harder, add ½ teaspoon xanthan gum when mixing in the liquid ingredients.

# measurement conversions

## VOLUME EQUIVALENTS (LIQUID)

| US STANDARD | US STANDARD (OUNCES) | METRIC (APPROXIMATE) |
|---|---|---|
| 2 tablespoons | 1 fl. oz. | 30 mL |
| ¼ cup | 2 fl. oz. | 60 mL |
| ½ cup | 4 fl. oz. | 120 mL |
| 1 cup | 8 fl. oz. | 240 mL |
| 1½ cups | 12 fl. oz. | 355 mL |
| 2 cups or 1 pint | 16 fl. oz. | 475 mL |
| 4 cups or 1 quart | 32 fl. oz. | 1 L |
| 1 gallon | 128 fl. oz. | 4 L |

## OVEN TEMPERATURES

| FAHRENHEIT (F) | CELSIUS (C) (APPROXIMATE) |
|---|---|
| 250°F | 120°C |
| 300°F | 150°C |
| 325°F | 165°C |
| 350°F | 180°C |
| 375°F | 190°C |
| 400°F | 200°C |
| 425°F | 220°C |
| 450°F | 230°C |

## VOLUME EQUIVALENTS (DRY)

| US STANDARD | METRIC (APPROXIMATE) |
|---|---|
| ⅛ teaspoon | 0.5 mL |
| ¼ teaspoon | 1 mL |
| ½ teaspoon | 2 mL |
| ¾ teaspoon | 4 mL |
| 1 teaspoon | 5 mL |
| 1 tablespoon | 15 mL |
| ¼ cup | 59 mL |
| ⅓ cup | 79 mL |
| ½ cup | 118 mL |
| ⅔ cup | 156 mL |
| ¾ cup | 177 mL |
| 1 cup | 235 mL |
| 2 cups or 1 pint | 475 mL |
| 3 cups | 700 mL |
| 4 cups or 1 quart | 1 L |

## WEIGHT EQUIVALENTS

| US STANDARD | METRIC (APPROXIMATE) |
|---|---|
| ½ ounce | 15 g |
| 1 ounce | 30 g |
| 2 ounces | 60 g |
| 4 ounces | 115 g |
| 8 ounces | 225 g |
| 12 ounces | 340 g |
| 16 ounces or 1 pound | 455 g |

## My Other Cookbooks

*Dairy-Free Gluten-Free Baking Cookbook:* An educational baking cookbook filled with 75 favorite baking recipes safe for anyone with celiac disease and a dairy intolerance. It is extremely educational on the various flours available and how to use them and has three recipes for the best gluten-free flour mixes to make at home.

*Gluten-Free Dairy-Free Cookbook:* This book is filled with 100 satisfying, family-friendly recipes. It includes meat, seafood, pasta, and vegetarian dishes the whole family will enjoy.

## Websites

**CELIAC DISEASE FOUNDATION:** Celiac.org
Learn everything you need to about this autoimmune disease and its effects. In studies, there is a link between gluten intolerance and dairy intolerance.

**FOOD AND DRUG ADMINISTRATION:** www.fda.gov/Food
Learn about how the Food and Drug Administration regulates foods and their food labeling so you and your family can stay safe.

**FOOD ALLERGY RESEARCH AND RESOURCE PROGRAM:** farrp.unl.edu
Get the latest research on the food industry related to food allergies.

**INSTITUTE OF AGRICULTURE AND NATURAL RESOURCES:** ianr.unl.edu
A resource for information on dairy, nondairy, lactose, and milk allergies.

**KIDS WITH FOOD ALLERGIES:** KidsWithFoodAllergies.org
A division of the Asthma and Allergy Foundation of America. Learn all about food allergies, signs, symptoms, and more.

**NATIONAL AGRICULTURAL LIBRARY: US DEPARTMENT OF AGRICULTURE:** www.nal.usda.gov/fnic/milk-allergies-and-lactose-intolerance
Educational facts about milk allergies, lactose intolerance, and more.

# references

American Academy of Allergy, Asthma & Immunology. "Allergy Statistics." American Academy of Allergy, Asthma & Immunology. aaaai.org/about-aaaai /newsroom/allergy-statistics.

American College of Allergy, Asthma & Immunology. "Milk & Dairy Allergy." American College of Allergy, Asthma & Immunology. Updated March 21, 2019. acaai.org/allergies/types-allergies/food-allergy/types-food-allergy/milk -dairy-allergy.

Food Allergy Research and Resources Program. "Allergenic Foods and Their Allergens, with Links to Informall: Milk." University of Nebraska—Lincoln Institute of Agriculture and Natural Resources. Updated March 10, 2014. farrp.unl.edu/allergenic-foods-and-their-allergens-links-informall.

Food Allergy Research and Resources Program. "Dairy-Free and Non-Dairy?" University of Nebraska—Lincoln Institute of Agriculture and Natural Resources. farrp.unl.edu/resources/gi-fas/opinion-and-summaries/dairy-free-and -non-dairy.

Food Allergy Research and Resources Program. "Prevalence of Food Allergies." University of Nebraska—Lincoln Institute of Agriculture and Natural Resources. farrp.unl.edu/resources/gi-fas/prevalence-of-food-allergies.

Groce, Victoria. "What Is a Dairy-Free Diet?" Verywellfit.com. Updated February 3, 2020. VeryWellFit.com/what-is-a-dairy-free-diet-1324040.

Indorato, Debra A. "Milk Allergy Avoidance List: Hidden Names for Milk." KidsWithFoodAllergies.org, March 2015. KidsWithFoodAllergies.org/media/Milk -Allergy-Avoidance-List-Hidden-Names.pdf.

National Dairy Council. "What Is Lactose?" December 20, 2017. National Dairy Council: News and Articles. USDairy.com/news-articles/what-is-lactose.

Porto, Anthony. "Lactose Intolerance in Infants and Children: Parent FAQs." HealthyChildren.org. American Academy of Pediatrics. Updated September 29, 2016. HealthyChildren.org/English/healthy-living/nutrition/Pages /Lactose-Intolerance-in-Children.aspx.

United States Food and Drug Administration. "What You Need to Know about Food Allergies." United States Food and Drug Administration. Updated September 26, 2018. www.fda.gov/food/buy-store-serve-safe-food/what-you-need-know-about-food-allergies.

US National Library of Medicine. "Lactose Intolerance." US National Library of Medicine: Genetics Home Reference. ghr.nlm.nih.gov/condition/lactose-intolerance.

# index

# acknowledgments

First of all, I have so much to be grateful for and so many people to thank (not necessarily in this order), so here we go! I want to thank you for getting this book, my readers. It is a joy to finally have it in your hands after months of recipe testing and writing with a drive to fuel families everywhere with tasty dishes children can enjoy without missing out on their favorite foods!

I thank my children, Chase and Curren. This book is especially for you boys, because you helped create it for all the children in the world. You bring so much joy to life and I appreciate your time coming up with recipe ideas and all your constructive criticism as we taste tested the recipes together. Even the ones we had to retry until you gave final approval.

To my loving husband, Kristopher, who supports me through everything and the hours I was checked out of housework to put this book together. I think I can say for everyone, we greatly appreciate the hours of folding laundry and helping me with endless dishes.

To my incredible publishing company, Callisto Media, and wonderful editor and the rest of our team. This book exists because of each of you. Thank you so much for your time, dedication, thorough editing, photography, Zoom chats, and so much more that is put into the production of making a book go from an idea to existence. You all rock and I truly love you all for it.

And always, to God, my Lord and Savior. You are everyday manifesting my dreams to come true. Thank you for life and all of its great opportunities.

# about the author

**DANIELLE FAHRENKRUG** is a healthy living, whole-food advocate dedicated to helping others regain and maintain their health and vibrance through healing, real food recipes. You can find her sharing recipes and tips on her popular blog *DelightfulMomFood.com*. She specializes in fueling families with delicious gluten-free recipes while educating readers on the benefits of the specific foods and ingredients in each recipe. You can also find her high-quality line of natural health supplements at DelightfulMomHealth.com. On social media, you will find her on Instagram, Facebook, and Pinterest (@DelightfulMomFood). She lives in California with her husband and two boys.

Printed in the USA
CPSIA information can be obtained
at www.ICGtesting.com
CBHW081246200224
4497CB00002B/7

9 781646 116225